Tricks of the
Trade

A Real Estate Broker's Inside Advice on
Buying or Selling a Home

BRENDAN J. CUNNINGHAM

ADAMS MEDIA
AVON, MASSACHUSETTS

This book is fondly dedicated to the three women in my life.
My mother, who taught me to never be ashamed of hard work and to
never take myself too seriously, and who paints in oils at age eighty-seven.
To my darling wife, Kathleen, who continuously inspires me,
and to my daughter, Alice, who always delights me.

Published by
Adams Media, an F+W Publications Company
57 Littlefield Street, Avon, MA 02322. U.S.A.
www.adamsmedia.com

ISBN: 1-58062-950-4

Printed in the United States of America.

J I H G F E D C B A

Library of Congress Cataloging-in-Publication Data
Cunningham, Brendan J.
Tricks of the trade / Brendan J. Cunningham.
p.   cm.
ISBN 1-58062-950-4
1. Real estate business--United States. 2. House buying--United
States. 3. House selling--United States. I. Title.
HD255.C87 2004
333.33'3'0973--dc21

2003004478

This publication is designed to provide accurate and authoritative information with regard to the subject matter covered. It is sold with the understanding that the publisher is not engaged in rendering legal, accounting, or other professional advice. If legal advice or other expert assistance is required, the services of a competent professional person should be sought.
—From a *Declaration of Principles* jointly adopted by a Committee of the American Bar Association and a Committee of Publishers and Associations

Many of the designations used by manufacturers and sellers to distinguish their products are claimed as trademarks. Where those designations appear in this book and Adams Media was aware of a trademark claim, the designations have been printed with initial capital letters.

This book is available at quantity discounts for bulk purchases.
For information, call 1-800-872-5627.

Contents

Chapter 1 The Tie That Binds:
The Real Estate Contract / 1

*The contract is the soul of the real estate transaction, though
few agents and consumers bother to really read it.*

Chapter 2 Salespeople, Brokers, Agents,
and the Whole Cast of Characters / 16

*Understanding the roles of these players can save you
money, time, and a lot of frustration.*

Contents

Chapter 13 Getting the Word Out: Newspapers, the Internet, and More / 160

The power—and the weakness—of newspaper advertising, along with some invaluable Web tools (especially for buyers)

Chapter 14 Buying and Selling: Rules to Live By / 174

Three dozen rules for buying and selling that will save you money now and in the future

Chapter 15 When You're in Trouble, Whom Should You Call? / 185

A step-by-step guide to what to do and whom to call when a deal goes wrong

Chapter 16 Getting Started / 193

Some last words of advice before you jump into the wonderful world of real estate

Acknowledgments

No great thing is ever accomplished alone. This book may not prove to be a great work for the ages, but writing has been a great thing for me, and it certainly was not accomplished alone. First, I must thank those who gave me guidance and assistance during my real estate career, starting with the first broker I was fortunate enough to associate with, and the man who sold me my first house, William Lockridge Harris of Renaissance Properties Ltd. I learned more from Bill than he could possibly realize.

One of the more valuable lessons I learned in the business came from Ruben Windmiller, who tragically died in 1996 on TWA Flight 800. I can still almost hear him say, in his thick Israeli accent, "The hardest thing to get a man to do is put his hand in his pocket and have him come out with money."

I also must thank Joanie Stovroff. Her love of the business gave me a new enthusiasm when I first arrived in Western New York. She took a chance on an unknown, and for that I will always be grateful.

Tom Cusack of the Cusack School of Real Estate and Professional Development has been a co-worker and friend for many years, and his helpful insights into the study of Neuro-Linguistic Programming and the subtleties of communication have proven invaluable.

Stuart Hunt reminded me, as only the most venerable man in the entire real estate world could, of the reason we are in business in the first place: "to make a profit." His son, Peter, likewise taught me about the value of a sound business plan and having the integrity to stick to it.

I also must extend appreciation to Floyd Wickman. He is one of the best trainers in the real estate business, and his tapes and seminars have inspired my path throughout my career. His philosophy is embodied in what he wrote in my personal copy of his book entitled *Mentoring,* something I have always tried to do: to build "success, helping people help themselves."

The penultimate words of gratitude must go to Brian Bertoldo, whose crafting of the copyedit for this book made what I think is an enjoyable book read even better. Copyeditors are the unsung heroes in the publishing world, and I would be truly remiss if I did not sing his praises here, regardless of how off key I might sound.

And a final thank you to Jill Alexander, also of Adams Media, who has been a delight to work with through the entire publishing process. She believed in me and the project from the get-go, and without her, *Tricks of the Trade* would not have become a reality.

Introduction

Why this book? When people ask me what I do for a living I have responded the same way for the last twenty-three years: "I'm a real estate broker." Many of my colleagues and associates usually mention the company that they work for, and then do what I call a "commercial" in the hope that a good thirty-second sell job might get them a lead or some business. Maybe it does. Me, I just tell them, "I'm a real estate broker."

Whenever I do that, people immediately have a flood of questions for me. If I then want to get away, I sometimes have my work cut out for me.

It's been a good life for me, because I'm good at what I do and I like what I'm doing. But another reason this business has been good to me is that I've always taken the high road. If the transaction didn't at first make sense for all parties concerned, I made sure that it did in the end.

There is an expression that one should look for win/win scenarios in all of our business dealings. Perhaps to some in this post-Enron world this appears old-fashioned. That's a shame. Because, unfortunately, you and I both know that there are some in the world of business, and even in my profession, who simply refuse to take the high road. They look to take short cuts, tell half-truths, manipulate the deal, and sometimes (I am sorry to say) do things that are at the least less than honorable and at the worst simply unethical.

In some extreme circumstances, some of their actions just aren't legal. In this book we will discuss many of these issues frankly. My purpose is not to condemn any of my peers (and certainly not the people in my own company). But, to be honest, there are some cooperating brokers I have known over the years who, if put under oath about their practices, might have to raise their hands and say,

"Guilty, your honor." My goal is to raise the standard of what we do in the real estate business and to help maintain and enhance it as the honorable profession I have always believed it to be.

Yes, dear readers, there *are* tricks of the trade. At the bare minimum there are techniques used in our business that, when used in less than honorable ways, really do become tricks. One of the things I remember from the earliest days of my selling career is that the difference between "a con and a sell" is only one thing: intention.

In one of my more doomed attempts to raise the standards in our business, I would remind new salespeople of the importance of eliminating four-letter words from their professional vocabulary. Words like "sell," for example. Is there anyone out there who likes to be "sold" on anything? (Oh, that's another four-letter word.)

Here's the word I would ask them to use instead: Help. Granted, it too is a four-letter word, but so is "love," and clearly these two elicit a more favorable response from each of us. Everyone wants "help," don't they? "Try not to sell," I would urge my staff. All that is required is that you find out what people want and then get out of their way and *help* them get it. That's the key. This book will help put you on guard against those nefarious individuals in the field who would use their powers for evil instead of for the good of us all. After you come to understand some of these insider tips, you'll be better able to work with brokers and more easily buy and sell your home.

I remember having a conversation with my brother Dennis. He is in the securities business and is also a broker— a stockbroker, that is. At the time, he was leaving a relatively large firm to go with another firm because of "philosophical differences." That's a phrase that's been worked to death, too. But in his case it was genuine. For this reason, I am willing to wager that regardless of what the market is doing, Dennis will always run a very respectable business.

The "differences" in Dennis's case stemmed from what one of his sales managers said. It had to do with the ultimate impact that a stock trade would have for the firm, the broker, and the client. Dennis knew it was time to move on when the manager glibly exclaimed, "Well, the company did well, you did well . . . two out of three isn't bad." If we are to have a profession of selling real estate, or securities, or widgets, then the two out of three mentality simply doesn't cut it—not with me and hopefully not with anyone reading this book. This includes agents, brokers, and people who are looking to work with either of them when buying or selling a home.

This book will also help you understand the different players in the transaction, what their relationship is, and how important it is for you to know and understand what each of their jobs are. You will learn how to read even the most complicated real estate contract because you will know what the essentials are and where to find them. The Talmud says that the Bible has one truth: Love God. The rest is commentary. I will teach you the five things to look for in *any contract*. The rest, likewise, is commentary.

Some questions I am asked all the time: Is this a good time to sell? Is this a good time to buy? Is this a good place to buy in? You will have the definitive answer amply covered in Chapters 3 and 4. You will also learn what hurdles you'll have to leap if you want to sell your own home yourself, or what to consider if you are thinking of buying a FSBO (for sale by owner).

In Chapter 7, you'll learn to be on your toes when you walk into the "Venus Fly Trap," also known as the Open House. If you're a potential buyer, you definitely should be on your guard. If you're an agent, you should read this chapter; maybe you'll learn a trick or two.

One of my favorite subjects is in Chapter 8: the wonderful world of negotiating and the shorthand or jargon you need to know. I call it the "talk of the town."

Picking an agent—whether you are buying or selling—is easy, if you know what to look for. I'll show you how in Chapter 9.

What should you know about home inspections? Do you need one? What are the sellers trying to hide? In Chapter 10 you will learn when you absolutely, positively should have an inspection, whom you should get, and how you should work it into the contract if you are the buyer or the seller. The answer is different depending on which side you're on in the transaction. There are many myths about this side of the business. You'll find out why home inspection is one of the fastest growing businesses in our country, even though it is, as yet, virtually unregulated.

Can you buy real estate with nothing down? *Absolutely!* I'll show you how, and give you more than a dozen ways to do it.

In addition, there is a lot you need to know about the customs, protocol, and law of the real estate business. Yes, it is important that "when in Rome" you act as the Romans do. It will certainly help you to understand what people say, and why they do what they do.

In Chapter 13 on newspapers and the Internet, you'll learn where to look for the best deals, and what real estate ads are "really" saying. When are advertisements legal? When are they not? What impact does the Internet have on the industry today, and what will it mean ten years from now?

Saving money . . . are you interested? Whether buying or selling, I'll give you thirty-six sure-fire strategies to help you skin the peel off that financial banana called the real estate transaction each and every time. It's not so hard. It just takes a little savvy and some of the helpful hints in this book. This one chapter alone could save you thousands of dollars in the short term, and maybe tens of thousands in the long run.

And lastly, whom are you going to call when you get in trouble? I'll give you insights and directions on finding "the people in the know" if you get in over your head. Hey, it could happen, even after you've read this book.

Real estate is a dynamic business. Sometimes, even armed with the best knowledge, the rules change on you. You should know what to do in those circumstances. This book can better equip you to deal with those problems that require picking up the phone and talking to the right party. But first you'll need to identify just whom it is you need to call to iron out the grievances that might arise from an unusual real estate transaction. However lost you might find yourself, with a few tricks and a few numbers we'll help get you back on track, or at least get you the proper recourse.

I've mentioned that I am a real estate broker. Let me give you a little more of my background. I got into the business as a result of buying my first house. At the time, I was a working actor in New York City and had just purchased a three-family home near the Brooklyn Heights section of Brooklyn in an artsy transitional neighborhood called Boerum Hill. For those of you who saw the movie *Moonstruck* with Cher and Nicolas Cage, it was shot in my backyard.

As my real estate career began, I was selling brownstones just like the ones in the movie. Having earned enough from some beer commercials, I was smart enough to buy a house in this really neat area that adjoined the best section in town. This brings up an invaluable insight: "Buy on the fringe and wait." I learned this because as it happens, one sunny afternoon the fellow who sold me my house caught me in the act of sweeping my stoop. I was giving directions to some friendly passersby, and I was explaining all about the neighborhood. "You should go down to the corner, make a left on Court Street, and go one block past Cusimano's bakery," and all in all I was really doing an incredibly animated selling job on the pleasures this particular little section of heaven had to offer.

Bill Harris, the broker who sold me my house, waited for a break in my monologue and asked me, "Hey, do you want a job?"

I said, "Doing what?"

He said, "Selling real estate."

I asked him, "What the hell do I know about selling real estate?"

He said, "Trust me kid, you're a natural."

In the next few years, I had the pleasure of working with Bill as a sales agent. I learned a lot about the business. He was a lawyer who didn't practice law but owned a small residential real estate firm with three offices in brownstone Brooklyn. It was the age of renovation and his company was appropriately named Renaissance Properties, Ltd. With the gas crisis and oil embargoes of the '70s, people were rediscovering neighborhoods that had been, in most cases, totally abandoned.

Bill is still working in the neighborhood, and he probably enjoys what he is doing as much now as when he started over thirty years ago.

For many people it made more sense to return to the city, grab up these vintage buildings, restore them to the grandeur of their nineteenth-century elegance, and quit commuting to places like Long Island and New Jersey. It made a lot of economic sense for a lot of people. As the quality of the housing stock was improved, fortunes were made by many, including my friend Bill. It was one of the more exciting times in my life. In some respects it was like a modern-day gold rush; speculation was rampant and it was not unusual to see shrewd investors buy buildings in the morning and "flip" them in the afternoon and make a quick forty or fifty thousand. Hey, it was the '80s—the decade of rampant inflation, 19 percent interest rates, and Reaganomics.

I didn't do too badly myself. More importantly, I made a lifelong friend in the process. It was a rollicking good time and the biggest winners came from those who bought and held the longest—more on that later in the chapter on "When is the right time to sell?"

After buying and selling a lot of properties of my own, I left the city. I sought a more pastoral life in a little town right out of a Norman Rockwell painting called East Aurora, seven miles east of Orchard Park, New York (which any football fan can tell you is the home of the Buffalo Bills).

Unfortunately, the pastoral life for me was interrupted by an almost insatiable lust for (you guessed it) the real estate business. In the last seventeen years alone, I have sold or managed the sales of well over a billion dollars in residential and commercial property. In the process I've learned what to do and what not to do. I've learned what to say and what not to say (and when not to say it). In short, I've learned when to hold 'em and when to fold 'em . . . and one thing's for certain, not all education comes easy.

In my career, I have worked for small companies and large companies. I've owned my own firm and been my own boss. I have been the sales and marketing director for various condominium and co-op projects as well as being involved in property management. I've written numerous articles and have had my own radio call-in talk show. From relocation to foreclosure, to the wonderful world of real estate auctions—it seems like every aspect of our business has come across my desk at one time or another. Note that I said it *seems*, because one of the neatest things about this business is that even though there are set patterns, every day is fresh with unexpected opportunities. It's one of the greatest jobs I can think of, and the best part is, it really is quite simple. All that is required is someone who wants to buy, and someone who wants to sell. That's it. It sounds straightforward enough, and it is. The journey between those two points is the part that, in most cases, is anything but simple.

That's where the work comes in, and that's where you come into the picture. Whether you are an agent, a broker, a buyer, or a seller, now is the time to come and join me as we take a magical mystery tour through the wonderful world of real estate. Who knows, you might learn a trick or two.

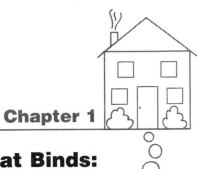

Chapter 1

The Tie That Binds:
The Real Estate Contract

Fasten your seat belts; it's going to be a bumpy night.
        —Bette Davis in *All About Eve*

To give you a better grasp of how the real estate business fits together, we need to find a starting point. First of all, as I have mentioned before, this is the simplest business I know. It is not necessarily an "easy" business. It is, however, a simple one. Along the way, all sorts of roadblocks and obstructions are thrown up by various players in an effort to keep willing buyers and willing sellers from coming together. Sometimes it is by design. Sometimes it is an accident. And sometimes it is through careful manipulation by either of the principals, the attorneys, or the real estate broker.

Because of this we need a map to guide us through the wilderness. Your best map to the real estate process is the real estate Contract of Sale. It is the single most important document in the real estate process.

However, for some strange reason, the contract is usually the last part of the process covered in most real estate training programs. The contract is the end, in a manner of

1

speaking, but it really should be the beginning. In most training programs, agents begin by learning how to qualify buyers. They learn the business of selling and how to make money and later move on to understanding the local "laws governing agency"—the relationship an agent has to the broker and the consumer. It is only *then* that they learn to understand and deal with the vicissitudes of the contract.

In my experience, though, it makes no sense to begin a trip if you have no idea where it will end. And arriving at the contract is certainly the desired destination of every journey in the real estate business. So let's begin there.

The Most Important Part of the Contract

The purpose of the sales contract is to bring parties together so that the agreement to buy and sell real property is clearly understood by all parties making the agreement. As such, the law requires that the contract be written down. There is, however, a phrase that I learned many years ago while I was still studying to come into this business. It may be the most valuable piece of information you'll ever get about the real estate business.

Here it is: *Oral agreements between principals and brokers are binding in a court of law.* That's right, oral agreements are, in fact, legally binding. Even for civilians—folks outside the real estate industry—this rule pretty much holds true. To protect the consumer, the law does, in just about every jurisdiction I know, require that contracts be written down. This requirement might just be to remind people what they said in the first place, though I sometimes suspect it is meant to provide written proof in order to prevent people from acting like weenies.

When I taught contracts to new folks coming into the business, I knew it was my job to never let them forget the most critical part of any real estate transaction. At the first class, I would hold up a blank contract and ask the question, "What's the most important part of the contract?" I would get several answers, each one valid in one respect or another. So I would rephrase it another way, "What is the most important issue that you deal with in the contract?" Now there were lots of answers.

"Get it in writing."

"The signature . . . yeah, it has to be signed by all parties."

"Get a big deposit."

As soon as the class started to run out of things to call out, I would take the blank contract, roll it into a tight ball, and throw it with a concentrated effort to hit someone as far away as I could, usually someone who was bigger than I was. Just as the paper hit some poor unsuspecting fellow on the top of the head, I would yell out, "The people making the agreement!"

It is the people, the individuals, entering into the agreement who are more important than any single sentence, clause, or paragraph in the contract. My little exercise has never failed to get my students' attention. And it is the simplest of concepts that are often the most profound.

To understand any contract, anywhere, in any state—from the most complicated commercial contract to the simplest residential purchase—there arc five essentials that have to be understood and identified immediately if there is to be any success for anyone involved in the transaction. I call it the five "Ps." They are the *parties*, the *property, the payment, possession*, and the *price*.

The Parties to the Contract

The first P refers to the *parties* or the *principals*. They are also known as the buyer and seller. When I first got into the business, Bill (the first broker I worked with) asked me to write an ad for a new listing I had just brought into the office. I had seen in another ad somewhere one phrase that really caught my attention and which I thought I would use in my ad. The phrase was, "principals only." I liked the way that sounded. It had panache. Bill reviewed the ad, as all brokers are required to do by law, and said, "Hey, great ad, but you're an agent, stupid. I presume you want other agents to show this property, don't you?"

You see, I thought that "principals only" meant that only serious buyers need apply, that only high rollers should bother responding. Wrong! Principals are the parties to the transaction: the buyer and the seller. The term is used to distinguish them from other people or individuals or entities that also might have an interest in the transaction. These might include agents, attorneys, banks, home inspectors, appraisers, life tenants, and remaindermen (I just love that term; see the glossary for an explanation), just to name a few.

Back to the classroom, where my students were still regaining their composure from the paper projectile. I would continue my tutorial on contracts and state, "Quite frankly, there isn't a contract out there that couldn't be broken by any self-respecting attorney that has a mind to do so. There might be some financial adjustments to be made out of any abortive attempt to scuttle a deal, but the point is, it can be done if that's what one or both of the parties want to have happen."

As I would expand on this point I would ask the class to consider our august government, the land of the free, In God We Trust, and so on. "Look at all the contracts, the treaties, we had with the Native Americans," I'd say. We had hundreds of them. Some are still on display in the Smithsonian. Look at all the contracts we broke with them. Willing parties? You bet. The government maybe even had some remote thought of keeping some of those agreements.

"And what about football?" I would then ask. Every year in late summer or early fall, I'd point out, it seems that there are always a group of crybaby players who want to hold out for more money even though they have a contract. By this point the room usually became very quiet.

"So what the hell good is it to even have a contract?" someone would finally ask, annoyed that a simple class on contracts had taken this turn.

"Just get over it," I'd say. "This isn't a perfect world . . . this is real estate." I wanted everyone to know that my message was 100 percent sincere, but that it wasn't always going to be sweetness and light. Sometimes the real estate business is not necessarily user-friendly. I got my students' attention by merely pointing out the harsh reality right up front.

Individuals, Not Ink, Make a Contract

To illustrate the importance of the first P, the people who make the agreement, let me pose a hypothetical contract. The terms are all agreed to, you've gotten the full price—in cash, and you can close whenever you want. What could be better?

Until one of the people involved speaks up: "Allow me to introduce myself. The name's Manson . . . Charles. My friends call me Charlie or Chuck for short." Obviously, at least one of the parties in this would-be transaction is not credible. No sale!

The core issue with the first P is credibility. Are the parties involved people of their word? What is the ultimate probability of them performing? If you can't make the agreement on a handshake (believe me, I am not advocating that you do), if the parties are not honorable and the weenie factor is high, we have what I will call a problematical sale. Remember one thing: All the paper in the world, and all the addenda you can muster, just aren't worth a damn if someone wants to—and I mean *really* wants to—weasel out of a deal. Ask any lawyer. Even if you ultimately win your case, with the time, money, and aggravation incurred you will always come out the loser.

Donald Trump gives a beautiful illustration of this point in his book, *Trump: The Art of the Deal*. Incidentally, I would recommend this book as required reading for any would-be real estate professional. Trump (who tells the story much better than I do) had decided to build his Trump Tower. The site that he selected was on prestigious Fifth Avenue, in the fifties overlooking Central Park, and of course the new tower would have blocked the view of some of its neighbors. It was therefore necessary for Trump to purchase the *air rights* from the owner of one of the nearby buildings. The building in question was the world-famous Tiffany's, which was owned at the time by a gentleman named Walter Hoving.

The deal was struck and the appropriate paperwork drawn up. The architects and construction people were lined up, but, unfortunately, Mr. Hoving went out of town before the deal had been "inked." Needless to say, "The Donald" became very much concerned, as a second bidder had now entered the picture and without those air rights there wouldn't be a Trump Tower, at least not on that site. Even more unnerving to Trump, the second bidder was willing to pay considerably more.

In the heartwarming ending to the story, Mr. Hoving revealed just what kind of a gentleman he was. Hoving rather sternly reminded Trump, then just a young upstart, that they had a deal and that there was no reason to be concerned just because he hadn't attended to the paperwork yet. Integrity is a wonderful thing. Even if someone was willing to pay an additional fifty million dollars, Mr. Hoving had given his word. That was good enough for him. The contracts were mere formalities.

Most people hearing this today would say "Wow." I certainly do when I hear stories like this. It would be really great if everyone kept their word as well as this. But they don't, so the next best thing is to get it on paper in something called a *contract*.

"P" Is for Property

The second P refers to the *property* itself. What goes with it, and what doesn't go with it? Is there any personal property included? As an interesting aside: Have you ever wondered what *real* property is anyway? Did you ever wonder why it is call *real*? As opposed to what, unreal?

"Real property," as it turns out, is derived from the words "royal property." Way back when, in the age of monarchies, all the lands far and wide were owned by the Crown and were subsequently bestowed on to worthy knaves who had proven their value by performing some service to the ruler.

So much for the abridged history lesson. The current definition refers to "land and its improvements." Personal property is all the other stuff you can remove or carry away with you. We could spend a lot of time on the various kinds of ownership and the theories of the same, such as fee simple, fee absolute, condominiums, etc. But it will save us all a lot of time if you would just refer to them in the handy glossary at the end of this book instead.

Okay, back to our hypothetical contract. All the terms are in agreement and this time the would-be purchaser is not a notorious cult leader and murderer. This time, however, the very credible buyer wants all of the personal property—attached, not attached, everything—included with the price. Based on the contents, you may or may not be able to comply, or you may choose not sell. In any event, you have a serious issue to reckon with before there can be that all-important meeting of the minds.

Sealing the Deal: Defining Payment and Terms

The third P refers to *payment*. Sometimes we call this the *terms*. How a party elects to pay for a property is sometimes the single most important part of the contract and the subject of the most intensive negotiations. Will it be cash, conventional financing, owner hold, land contract, or what? If it is to be an owner-held mortgage, what are the terms of the payout? Is there a balloon payment? Will the mortgage be self-amortizing? What is the rate? Is the mortgage assumable? If so, do the terms stay the same? If it involves vacant land, is there a provision for sub-dividing? Does the mortgage stipulate a release clause?

These are just some of the many points to consider when we are dealing with how payment in its entirety is to be made. What about the earnest money deposits? Are they substantial enough for the seller? These issues can be a dealmaker or a deal killer.

Many times in the late '70s and early '80s, when interest rates were approaching 19 percent, attractive owner-held deals went together with below-market rates when it would have been inconceivable to sell properties any other way. The hackneyed rule of location, location, location simply didn't cut it back then; instead, the rule was terms, terms, terms. I still maintain that I will buy any property you can find for me, right now, as long as I can name the terms. I would pay a million dollars for a house valued at only $65,000 if I choose my own terms. How about a dollar down and a dollar a week? Sounds like a good deal to me.

Possession of the Property

The fourth P refers to something that can often make or break a deal after all other terms have been successfully negotiated. Many times this term is confused with the closing date, or the date established for settlement, or the time when title is transferred. This is something I call *possession*.

Note: *Possession* and *closing* are not always the same. They can be, and more often than not, they are. They just don't have to be. In such cases where the contract stipulates that they are not, transactions can become problematical and sometimes impossible.

Let's return to our imaginary contract. All the terms are agreed to, but the buyer needs immediate occupancy. This could be a problem. Would it be prudent for you, the seller, to allow somebody to occupy the premises prior to closing? Moreover, how wise would it be to let someone move in prior to having a firm letter of commitment from the designated lender? Not very, perhaps. But if the purchaser insisted that this was the only way they could buy the property, what would you do? Obviously you would think about it seriously and would consult with your attorney who would advise you of the risks of such a venture. If there is some delay or unwillingness on the purchaser's part to close on time you, Mr. and Mrs. Seller, may become what we call landlords. There are many worse things to be, but if you wanted to be a seller and not a landlord the issue of possession could be a critical one for you.

Money Makes the Contract Go 'Round

The fifth P is usually—but not always—the most important. It is, of course, the *price*. In this "show me the money" world that we live in, many sellers have blinders up for anything but the price. Most of the time that's okay. But remember what I said before: I would buy any property, anywhere, at any price, as long as I could name the terms. My offer still stands. It is important to underscore this key issue, however. It would be fair to state that many local markets in the United States right now are clearly buyers' markets. The old notion of "location, location, location"—which changed to "terms, terms, terms" in the '80s—now seems to have shifted to "price, price, and price." Now more than ever we are witnessing just how mobile our society is willing to be if it can obtain a better price elsewhere.

Consider what is happening in the Carolinas, both North and South. Look at the incredible growth of Las Vegas. Now granted, places of this sort are attracting buyers for a myriad of reasons, but the single biggest lure is affordable housing, also known as *price*. With many northern states currently taxing their citizens to death, thousands are fleeing south to reduce their overall total monthly costs, which is an indirect way of saying that they want to pay a lower price. It is sad but true, and because of it we are seeing a redistribution of our nation's greatest resource, our next working generation. They are willing to go where housing is more affordable and are even willing to sever family roots to do so. Some would call it progress, but that is for you to decide.

So now you know the essentials of any real estate contract. The five Ps: the *people*, the *payment*, the *property*, *possession*, and the *price*. Many times when agents are presenting an offer they will blow some smoke in an effort to make the deal sound more attractive. Through carefully minimizing the importance of one of these core issues, the agent can create a sufficient cloud in an unsuspecting seller's mind as to what is really transpiring. Oh, the buyer is a great guy, and he is taking the property as is, and the seller will make an incredible amount of interest on this owner-financed deal. There's just one small problem: The buyer is willing to pay only one-fourth of what the property is worth! Or worse, he is willing to pay full price and possession is at the seller's discretion, and he is not asking for the crystal chandelier, but there isn't a banker in his right mind who would lend this bum a dollar under any circumstances!

The lesson? Read your contract and keep your eye on all of these essentials, and you will almost always come out just fine.

Beware of the Weasel

What is a weasel? In a contract, it is not a small hairy varmint in the woods. Much like our elusive furry friend, though, a determined buyer or seller can find clauses in any contract that provide holes through which he can escape and be on his merry way without recourse for the opposing party. Really savvy (and sometimes even unsavory) buyers or their agents put lots of weasel clauses in a contract to allow themselves every opportunity to back out for any reason.

In one common example of this practice, the contract is "subject to" approval by any third party. This can be an attorney, a spouse, a mother-in-law, an engineer, a home inspector, an architect, a building inspector, or a zoning board of review. These are always weasel clauses. It is not uncommon for buyers to put bids on multiple properties to see which will net the best deal. They make each bid "subject to" attorney review, then kill the less attractive sales and have their attorney approve the one they like the best. This can be structured to be legal, but it sure does a head job on the sellers who lost out. They thought they had a sale subject to a rubber stamp approval.

So what is the solution? There isn't one. There is, however, a counterstrategy. You can do what I call "contain the weasel" by putting very specific limitations on just how far you are willing to let him run. You want "attorney approval?" Fine . . . but for seventy-two hours, not three business days. Home inspector approval within the same period, not two weeks. You must look at each case and make a decision that makes sense for not just one side but for all parties involved. Remember, you have to "keep yourself covered at all times," just as if you were in the boxing ring.

The buyer, by the way, is almost always the one who initiates weasel clauses. Why is that, you say? It's simple— the seller wants to sell. Even if he is not extremely motivated, the seller is trying to put as few obstacles in the way of a speedy closing as possible. It is the buyer who in most cases is guilty of trying to manipulate the situation to the maximum advantage. Years ago we all learned about *caveat emptor.* (This used to be the only Latin you were required to know if you wanted to purchase real estate.) It means "Let the buyer beware." In this consumer age, the pendulum has indeed swung to the opposite extreme. It really should now be: "Let the seller beware." The point of this book is to let you know what you, as buyer *or* seller, should be aware of if you decide to play the game.

What Happens to the Money If Things Go Wrong

Another possible clause you must know about involves what are called *liquidated damages.* The simplest way of understanding this concept is "put up or shut up." If you put up X number of dollars to go to contract on a specific piece of property, what happens if you don't close? If it turns out that you breach the contract, what happens to the money you put up as an earnest money deposit or a down payment?

Depending on the contract, the clause covering this possibility can be liberal in favor of the buyer, the seller, or neither. When people agree to sell, everyone hopes to close and live happily ever after. But what if one of the parties has a change of mind? Believe me, it happens all the time. The solution to this dilemma lies in the specifics of the "liquidated damages" clause. Find it in the contract. It is crucial. Once the deal is struck, moneys are held in escrow pending the future closing. You need to know how those moneys are to be disbursed should there be an unforeseen "breach."

I live in Erie County, New York. In this neck of the woods, as in many other parts of the country, agents are allowed to fill in standardized contracts of sale that have been approved for use by the local real estate association and by the state bar association. Let's look at the "liquidated damages" clause contained therein.

Paragraph 11 states that *"if a written mortgage commitment for this mortgage is not received by the Purchaser by the_____ day of _____ 20__ either purchaser or seller may cancel this Contract by written notice to the other and the entire deposit (less survey certification) shall be returned. The same shall apply if the commitment is granted but later canceled without the fault of the Purchaser."*

Wait a minute, that's not it. That tells us what happens if the purchaser doesn't get his mortgage. He gets away scot-free in that case. It must be another clause.

Paragraph 14 states that *"if Purchaser finds valid objections to Seller's title which makes it unmarketable, Purchaser shall . . ."* accept it, or do something else. The something else is *"have the deposit returned to him together with reimbursement from the Seller for any nonrefundable fees paid by Purchaser, etc."*

Fair enough, but that's for situations where there is objection to title. What about a situation where the purchaser just willfully changes his mind? If the seller chooses not to close, the purchaser might go ahead and sue for specific performance. But what recourse does the seller have? He should at the minimum keep the deposit as liquidated damages, shouldn't he?

Guess what—nowhere in this contract that has been approved for use by a state bar association and a local Realtor association does it once mention who gets the down payment in the event of a breach of contract. This is a fine example of a Contract of Sale that is extremely user-friendly . . . if you happen to be a buyer. In Erie County, New York, buyers walk all the time, much to the chagrin and disappointment of sellers.

There are other ways to disguise a weasel. Look at the key dates set forth in any contract you're considering. How much time has been provided to get a mortgage or the various approvals? Are those dates reasonable or are they too long? What makes sense for your needs? You may find this amazing, but if you really stop to think about them specifically, the dates in a contract sometimes make absolutely no sense at all.

An example of this is a case from New York State where a contract stipulated that the buyer was going to get mortgage approval (thus requiring a formal letter of commitment) from a VA (Veterans Administration) mortgage in one week. This could have happened, conceivably, but in reality the time allowed was totally unrealistic. Most likely that buyer would be "out of contract" by day eight, and you—the seller—would have to chase him to get him to sign an addendum granting an extension.

You may be thinking to yourself, well, that is what I have an agent or an attorney for. Here is another shocker for you. In the situation I have just presented, the contract is perfectly legal and binding from the attorney's standpoint. The lawyer is not in the mortgage business and may not know how long it takes to cut through the governmental red tape of a VA mortgage. His only concern is to cast a legal opinion. The agent who filled in the blanks may have either not known how long it normally takes, or he may have tried to oversell the qualifications of the buyer.

Another possibility exists, and that is that the agent just goofed. Hey, it happens. And when it happens there are solutions that are reasonable . . . sometimes. It is situations just like this that require most agents to pay for something called errors and omissions insurance. That's just a little something they pay for in the wild stretch of the imagination that they may have to, on occasion, say "Oops," and that there are damages to pay to either a buyer, or in this case a seller.

It's All in the Contract

The Contract of Sale supersedes all other documents and agreements leading up to settlement or closing. Read it. (It never ceases to amaze me how few people do.) If you don't understand specific language in the contract, ask to have it explained to you so that even your nine-year-old could figure it out. A lot of the stuff in a contract is made deliberately difficult to understand just so you will have to have someone explain it to you. Maybe you wouldn't need to pay experts to do the explaining if they would just make the contracts easier. Oh, I know, now you are going to tell me about "Plain English" contracts. Yeah, right.

Here is the most important thing for you to take away concerning the Contract of Sale. As I've told you, it is, without a doubt, the most important document in the real estate transaction. Let me underscore one point so that there isn't any room for confusion. The Contract of Sale (with whatever number of riders) contains the *entire agreement* between the seller and the purchaser and *nothing* is binding for either of them that is not contained and explicitly spelled out in the contract. So don't go telling anyone after the fact that the agent said this, or the seller said that, unless you want to open a whole Pandora's box full of troubles. If you have a question or a requirement with respect to the purchase, put it in the contract, if you know what's good for you.

Chapter 2

Salespeople, Brokers, Agents, and the Whole Cast of Characters

The play's the thing . . . —Hamlet

To assemble a sales contract, and to bring about that all-important "meeting of the minds" in a real estate transaction, requires a monumental effort of people working together in concert. To bring a sale off without a hitch, so that there is not the slightest smattering of bloodshed on the closing room floor, takes an ensemble performance from a number of key players—or it takes an awful lot of luck. All too often it takes both. Some readers out there may be saying, "Are you kidding? I sold a house myself and it was as easy as pie." I could not be happier for those few fortunate individuals who have had that delightful experience. They are the exceptions that, as they say, prove the rule. Here's how it looks for the rest of us—the other 95 percent.

The sale starts when two opposing forces in the universe start to drift toward one another. We call them the buyer and the seller. Most often, a seller will decide that it makes sense to enlist the skill of a reputable broker to undertake the sale of a property. Soon—it is hoped—after this happens another party will come along and decide they need to buy a particular piece of property, usually at the behest of an agent who may or may not work for or with the original agent and who may or may not know anything about this property.

After determining what the person wants to buy, the agent searches through various information-gathering media and locates a suitable property based on what is known in the trade as a *needs determination*. The buyer is introduced to the property, price and terms are established, and there is agreement. Voilà—we have a sale. Sounds pretty simple, right? Let's take a closer look to see how it sorts out in the real world.

Now depending on what part of the country you are in, someone will prepare a Contract of Sale, also known as a *purchase agreement*, and will probably ask you for money. That person may be an agent, working with or for the buyer. That particular agent may instead just give the information over to the buyer's attorney and let him or her prepare it. The initial *earnest money* deposit, together with any subsequent down payments, will sit in an escrow account and will remain there until it is dispersed to the seller either through the escrow agent, the attorney working for the seller, or the seller's original agent.

In the unusual case where the property doesn't close as scheduled, those moneys may be deemed as liquidated damages (as was discussed in the previous chapter) or may be parceled out in some other way that is deemed equitable by the principals and/or the courts. If any of this sounds confusing, please hang in there. It will be as clear as mud in a moment.

Assembling the Cast of Characters

First we must consider the personnel we've assembled so far. We have two agents—one for the buyer and one for the seller. In some cases, the same agent can actually be working with the buyer and the seller, but this is less than typical. We have two attorneys (usually one for each principal). Then there are the principals themselves—let's not forget them. That's six people and we haven't even discussed the minor players in the supporting cast. Who are they?

The two agents in question probably work for different brokers and were originally linked up by something called a multiple listing system, which is nothing more than a formal agreement that allows a network of agents to cooperate together and share information. Here's an important aside. Whenever you work with an agent or a broker, they are, in fact, really not in the real estate business at all. At least not in the way you think. They do not actually sell you a house or get your house sold (unless they own the property themselves). What they actually do is bring about an event, which causes title to transfer between different parties. They do this by brokering or selling information, which leads to this event.

So we have added two more people, the brokers, who brought all this together by virtue of some "unilateral agreement of subagency" or cooperation. Okay, now we are up to eight individuals involved in the transaction. By the way, if all goes well you will never meet the brokers or even speak to them, unless things start to get very screwy.

These days chances are that the buyer will want to have the property inspected by an independent third party to decide if the parcel is in suitable condition to warrant a purchase or to determine what sort of deferred maintenance will be necessary in the succeeding years. This third party is called the home inspector. His job is to cast an opinion as to condition, not to value. That job goes to someone else.

Let's presume that this is a typical transaction and requires financing from a bank. The bank wants to protect its interests so they will order an appraiser (this is the guy who inspects for value) to be sent out to check out the property. His fee will be passed on to the purchaser. Presto!

We have just added three other involved parties to the list.

Now if you are in an area that requires various health certifications (for wells and/or septic systems), you might need to add two more inspectors. That's eleven people already! We could easily add two to five more if we take in inspections for the following: radon, water quality, termites, various kinds of molds, and lead paint contamination. So the number is somewhere between ten and fifteen individuals who must come together to complete what started out as one person deciding to sell and another deciding to buy. It sounded simple enough and it is. It is simple as sending a space shuttle into space and bringing it back without incident. Most of the time that's what happens. And sometimes somebody gets a call that goes something like the following: "Hello, Houston . . . we have a problem."

What could go wrong? The possibilities are as numerous as the stars in the heavens. So let's look at some of the "what ifs."

Playing Twenty Questions

Here's a list of questions that you might need answers for if you are to get any sleep once you have gone to contract.

1. Suppose the buyer is scheduled to bring in a second deposit after the binder or earnest money deposit has been collected and they simply forget to show up with the money. Is the deal dead?
2. How much time do you allow for the attorney to chase the buyer for the additional funds? Or is that the agent's job?
3. Whose escrow account should these moneys be deposited into: the seller's attorney, the listing agent, or an escrow agent?
4. Does the account draw interest, and if so, who is entitled to that interest?

5. Suppose the property is appraised for less than the contract sales price? Is the deal dead? Does the offer get renegotiated?
6. Can you appeal an appraisal?
7. If the appraisal is just an opinion of value, who gets to decide if the appraiser is right or wrong?
8. Suppose the buyer doesn't get his mortgage commitment in time, should the seller give him additional time? How much time is reasonable?
9. If the buyer has been prequalified for a loan, could he be turned down for the loan after he applies?
10. Can a buyer lose a commitment after a bank has issued one?
11. What if the buyer refuses to close on the date specified?
12. What does "time is of the essence" really mean? When should a buyer or a seller be concerned if they see that phrase in a contract?
13. If there is substantial damage to a property prior to a sale, what happens to the sale? Is the contract still valid?
14. Either the buyer or the seller dies prior to closing or settlement. What happens?
15. After closing, the purchaser (now the owner) discovers a serious structural defect that he is convinced the seller must have known about, but did not in fact disclose. What are the remedies?
16. The purchaser can't close on the property because of some serious personal circumstances. Does he have a way to legally extricate himself from the sale?
17. Title problems become obvious prior to closing. What happens? Whose problem is it?
18. You discover the fence separating the property is ten feet on the neighbors adjoining yard. What to do?
19. The assumable mortgage on the property turns out to be not assumable. What can be done to save the deal?
20. If any of these problems arise, who is the first person to call?

These are questions that you should research and educate yourself about. (Reading this book is a good start.) However, I'll answer the last and most important question for you right now. The first person to call if any of the above occurs is the agent or the broker with whom you are working. (The answers to the remaining questions can be found in Chapter 12.)

Whom to Call If the Road Gets Bumpy

You may have decided to go it alone as a seller and become what is known in the trade as a FSBO (it's pronounced FIZZ-BO and stands for "For Sale By Owner"). In that case, you can call your attorney and hope he or she returns your phone calls. If you are a buyer acting without the benefit of an agent, you can do the same thing. I'll wager that the situation is going to be a lot scarier for you since this is probably the first time you have bought a house, and you don't have a clue what to expect. At least the seller has gone through the purchase process before. You are going to have to listen to every friend and acquaintance who has ever bought a house, and they will almost always give you a lot of free—but bad—advice.

So what did I say before? Should you call the agent or the broker? You should call the person you were initially working with. No matter what their specific status, they are agents first and foremost. If they are salespeople it just means that they work for a broker. The broker is the owner of the company. There's a different license for that title and more elaborate training to obtain that distinction. Beyond that there really isn't that much of a difference. If you think you are not getting the right answers from your salesperson you can always ask to speak to the boss (the broker). Surprisingly, most (though not all) of your problems can be solved on your first call.

Invariably, what is perceived to be a major problem by

you is usually nothing, a glitch at best, something they have solved time and time again. Agents and brokers are quite accustomed to having disgruntled clients and customers calling (at all hours of the night, unfortunately) and saying terrible things to them.

Agents do two things: They act as conduits of information (they are information brokers), and they solve problems. Incidentally, you should pray that the agent has the answer or the solution to the problem. If the attorney has to solve it, it could cost you serious money. If he has to take it to court, it will cost you more than you ever bargained for. Your agent's solution is almost always your best bet and it will cost you the least. His fee has been set and he is more than likely being paid as a condition of the transaction. Agents usually only get paid if the sale closes, and thus they will do anything within their power to get the property closed and all parties satisfied.

One exception to the rule is the rare case where a buyer has hired a buyer's broker specifically and has elected to pay him on an hourly basis. If you are such a buyer you have just reaffirmed my belief in the expression, "There is a sucker born every minute." Don't pay up front for what you can get just about anyone in the business to do on a contingency basis.

Buyer Brokerage

Now that we have opened the Pandora's box of brokerage and clients, let's delve a little deeper. Traditionally, all agents have worked for the sellers. If you bought a house through an agent, they treated you as a customer. The buyer was almost never the client, the seller was. As such, under every state's regulations, they had an obligation to treat all parties fairly. They couldn't lie to you. They could not cheat or deceive you. If they did, there were strict penalties that could include a loss of license as well as fines and/or imprisonment. But, in almost all cases, the buyer was never the client. So the buyer did not have anyone working for him or representing his or her interests.

Enter the phenomenon of the '90s: *buyer brokerage.* These days, if you are the buyer you can have someone represent you, and you alone. You can have an agent who not only works with you like before, but also one who works *for* you like you are the client. That's pretty nifty, huh? And what's even better is that if you structure it correctly, you can have your very own agent *and* you can get the seller to pay for it. Now if all of this sounds a little too cool for words, maybe it is and maybe it isn't. What's important for you to know is that there is a difference between a buyer's broker and a seller's broker, and it is not just who gets to work with or for somebody. It has to do with two key words: *client* and *customer.*

Who is a client? A client is someone to whom an agent owes a fiduciary responsibility. An agent is defined as anybody who is empowered to perform a service for someone else; an example is the case of an attorney being the agent for a client with his particular role being to represent his client in legal matters. When a person is a fiduciary, that person acts for another in a relationship that involves great trust and due diligence.

A client receives other benefits from this very clearly established relationship, and agents are taught to remember those obligations through an acronym, which is referred to often by their brokers. The acronym is OLD CAR. The duties owed to a client by a fiduciary are:

Obedience
Loyalty
Due diligence
Confidentiality
Accountability
Reasonable care

Typically the agent works for the seller and is obligated to not only get his clients the best price and terms, but to also ensure that they receive all of the above. Where this could cause a problem is in the situation where a would-be purchaser might say, "Offer him a hundred, if he doesn't accept it, tell him I'll go to one fifteen." A seller's agent owes the fiduciary responsibility of confidentiality to the seller, not to the buyer. In this case the agent would be legally obligated to disclose the fact that the buyer would offer the higher price if necessary—thereby undermining the buyer's intentions to try to get the property for the lower price if possible.

Agents should decide for whom they are willing to work for based on the policies of the broker. They then should disclose that information at the first "substantive contact" that they might have with individuals they might come into contact with during the process. The term "substantive contact" could take volumes to define and is often the subject of great debate when an agency dispute arises. Let's give you two simple examples that should explain it without the entire fanfare.

Substantive contact occurs when an agent has a significant or a meaningful discussion whereby information of a personal or confidential nature is exchanged. What is meaningful? That is where the debate begins. Most of us can probably determine in our own minds what confidential means, so we'll skip that. The second way we can define "substantive contact" is to use what Supreme Court Justice Potter Stewart famously said when seeking to define whether something was pornography: "I know it when I see it." This definition works for me every time.

Because we live in an age of consumerism, and because many question the "fairness" in a real estate transaction, there are those who say all buyers should have their own representation and their own (buyer's) agent. This situation underscores something that we previously mentioned in passing.

If you are not a client you must be a customer (unless you're the agent, of course). Agents have an additional obligation to treat all parties fairly, especially their customers. After all, if agents don't treat their customers fairly, where will their future business come from?

Here's an important premise to grasp about this whole agency quagmire. A venerable gentleman whom I have had the wonderful opportunity to work for, Mr. Stuart Hunt, said it best at a sales meeting. Stuart is a second-generation chairman of the board for a very prestigious firm that was established in 1911, one which coincidentally bears his name. He got up one day and asked a group of top agents a simple question: "Why are we in business?"

The agents fired back a variety of answers:

"To serve the public."

"To sell houses."

"To be the best real estate company in town." (Some real brown-noser said this last one.)

"To earn commissions."

"To list and sell homes."

"To make money."

Now Stuart is not only venerable, but he is also the sweetest guy you'd ever want to meet. He patiently waited for a lull in the responses, and he then pounced back with the correct answer: "To make a profit." Never forget this one fact. You don't get to have a successful business from generation to generation without making a profit. Good service may be a given, but a profit is not. This is true for the real estate business as well, which means that there might be some agents that are not in it for the long haul but are looking to make the quick buck instead.

To offer a greater defense against these wily characters we will consider in Chapter 9 whether or not you should opt for a buyer's agent. There are "pros" and "cons," and believe me when I say that there is no pun intended here at all.

Working with Lenders

After the transaction is made, the ball is then passed to the lender—presuming that we are talking about a situation other than cash. (How many average Joes and Janes can buy a home outright anyway?) There are all kinds of lenders out there. Some are banks or credit unions. Some are relatives, and that's okay, too. Then there are other players called mortgage brokers and mortgage bankers. Let's consider each of these, except for the relatives; I'll just presume that you know who they are.

Credit unions are like banks with exclusive memberships. If you happen to be a member of a union (e.g., a teachers union) or a trade association, you can sometimes get incredibly favorable loan rates that are simply not available to the general public. With a credit union, much like with American Express, membership has its privileges. Always check with your credit union if you belong to one.

If you are not a member of one, proceed to banks via a *mortgage broker*. "Mortgage brokers" and "mortgage bankers" are a little different and demand a bit more explanation. The simplest way to describe these two is to say that they function exactly like travel agencies. If you wanted to fly Southwest Air to Florida, you could call the carrier directly. You could also call your travel agent who might book the flight or instead say to you, "Now there is another flight on Continental leaving half an hour later that is 10 percent less; would that work for you as well?"

The point is that with a travel agent you get other choices, and sometimes they can get you a better deal because they are able to shop the market better than you can. Also, it doesn't cost you a dime extra because the carrier pays their fee, not you. Brokers and bankers act exactly the same way. I could walk into my bank tomorrow and get a great deal on a mortgage (I've been a customer there for nearly thirty years). But you know what, the mortgage broker or mortgage banker can get me the same deal. The best part is, it won't cost me a penny more. In fact, it might even wind up saving me money. Please note, the broker cannot get me a better rate or fewer points than the specific bank is quoting on any given day, but they might get me a better deal with a different carrier.

They can also save me money because maybe my application would have been denied if I approached the bank directly. Perhaps my credit wasn't as good as I thought it was. Or maybe I just happened to forget about that bankruptcy a few years back. By that point, I might have incurred some fees that are nonrefundable. With a mortgage broker, the loan package can be resubmitted to another bank that may have a better program or more reasonable guidelines. There will be no additional fee for this, even if it is submitted to two or three lending institutions.

That's just the way it works. Always, I repeat *always*, work with a mortgage broker or a mortgage banker. It is not only a smarter way to do business, but the individual taking the loan application is on a commission, too; they don't get paid if they don't get a mortgage for you. Thus, they are highly motivated to get you a loan. They want to build a solid business for themselves as well, and they can't do that if they offer you bad service.

You are probably asking by now, what's the difference between a mortgage broker and a mortgage banker? It is a small one, but it might prove to be very important to you. A broker can only place loans with outside lenders. They can't actually lend you money. A mortgage banker can. They can actually choose to underwrite a mortgage themselves if they elect to do so. In addition, they can get direct endorsement for certain kinds of governmental loans—for example, FHA (Federal Housing Administration) mortgages. Brokers, in most instances, have to take an extra step to get these kinds of loans approved, which means additional paperwork for them, and inevitable delays for you. In a nutshell, all mortgage bankers are brokers but not all mortgage brokers are bankers. Choose a mortgage banker over a broker if you have the choice.

Here's another piece of strategy with respect to the lender. If the mortgage broker (or banker) is affiliated with the real estate broker you are working with, it is even better for you. This is because you have "increased leverage" in the transaction. This is true for both buyer and seller because the two firms will be earning additional commissions as a result of the sale. The mortgage broker will derive a fee from the lender and the real estate broker will earn a commission from the transaction itself. By the way, who pays (buyer or seller) will also be covered in Chapter 9. In the case above, both the mortgage and the real estate brokers have a larger vested interest in getting the transaction closed. This could come in handy if there is a crunch right at the end.

The lender, regardless of how he was obtained, will send someone out to represent his or her interest. This is the appraiser. His job is to make sure the property is worth whatever you have deemed fit to pay so that the bank's money (collateral) is secure. The property must appraise for the purchase price or higher in order for the lender to grant the buyer a formal commitment letter. There are exceptions in cases of refinancing properties, but, in general, these are the guidelines for purchase.

When the Property Doesn't Appraise

I love it when I see ads or highlight sheets on homes that indicate "priced below appraised value." Yeah, so what? That's the way it is supposed to be. If the property sells for more than what the property was appraised for there is a problem. Would you pay more for a property than the appraiser said it was worth? Most people wouldn't. In those rare instances four possibilities arise:

1. The sale doesn't go through at all.
2. The seller has to reduce the price to accommodate the difference between the sale price and the appraised price.
3. The purchaser has to take additional moneys out of his pocket that they might have wanted to use elsewhere, to make up the difference.
4. The difference is negotiated and the seller and purchaser come up with a compromised price.

Another alternative is to appeal the appraisal. After all, the appraiser is human and is doing nothing more than offering an opinion as to value. But remember, their opinion has more weight than most because of the training and various certifications that make them more or less an expert in this field. The value deemed to be appropriate is not just done on a P.F.A. basis. (P.F.A., by the way, is an insider expression that means "Plucked From Air.") No, the appraiser determines the value of the property based on what is called the Comparative Sales Approach. Using this method, the appraiser selects a minimum of three similar properties (e.g., three homes with similar square footage, number of bedrooms and baths, lot size, age, neighborhood, etc.). He notes what they sold for, and comes up with an accurate measurement of market value.

Many sellers will object to this method and maintain that "the people across the street are asking $50,000 more for their house than ours. Ours is much better and should be worth more." All of this is very interesting at a cocktail party but has nothing to do with the real world. The appraiser is only concerned with properties that have actually sold and closed. Something else that could mean additional bad news for you: In most cases their search will be limited to the last six months. So if you have the best house on the street and the market has been depressed all around you, your appraisal will be affected and could wind up costing you serious dollars.

We will discuss the home inspector in greater detail in Chapter 10, but he should not go without mention here. Very often an independent home inspector will be called in to render an opinion as to the overall condition of the property. He can be a saint or a deal killer. The important thing to remember for now is that their opinion is rendered with respect to condition alone—not price. The price opinion is the domain of the appraiser, not the home inspector.

Many first-time homebuyers discover a fault with the property shortly after closing and they want to string up the appraiser. He's the wrong party to go after in this case. Either party in the transaction can hire the home inspector, but usually the buyer is more concerned about the condition of the property prior to making the decision to buy than the seller is. The need for a third party to endorse that decision is the main reason for the entrance of the home inspector. As an aside, many a deal has gone awry when the home inspector holds the additional credential of being an appraiser and forgets which job he was actually hired to perform. When this happens, the word "Yikes" is often heard emanating from just about everyone concerned.

Depending on what part of the country you are in, it may be necessary to call in several other kinds of inspectors. Their expertise could involve inspecting for termites, radon, electro-magnetic fields, water quality, and septic and sewer. These additional inspections can be at the request of the purchaser or in some cases by the lender.

Working with Attorneys

In many communities, attorneys also play a big part in our little drama. However, if they screw up their role the results can often look more like a comedy. The thing is, you just can't escape them. The seller will have an attorney. The buyer will have an attorney. The bank will usually have one, too.

Sometimes the bank's attorney will make himself available to handle the purchaser's end of the deal as well. Of course, they won't do this for free. Many people frown upon this practice because of an implied conflict of interest between the bank and the buyer. I believe this conflict to be theoretical at best, and in the real world it probably makes more sense to do it this way. It can wind up saving the buyer some money because the buyer almost always assumes the cost of the bank's attorney anyway.

The attorney's job is really to make sure that title passes form one party to another without a hitch. Their opinions are in fact supposed to be restricted to rendering legal interpretations. Many times lawyers will use the phrase, "I approve the contract as to form and legal merit but not as to substance." Their expertise in the legal arena may equal F. Lee Bailey's, but in most cases they know little to nothing about what current market conditions are. If they did, they would be practicing real estate brokers instead of lawyers.

Here's another aside: In virtually all fifty states, attorneys are automatically real estate brokers, or at least they get the credential to say that they are. Because of this, a strange paradox arises. Attorneys are not really supposed to tell you that you paid too much or sold for too little (unless they are actually in the business on a day-to-day basis, that is.) If they render an opinion as to value, and they are not in the business, they're just showing off and don't know what they are talking about. But, guess what. They usually do talk too much, and many times they will kill deals for no apparent reason simply because their client asks them to do so. (This sometimes occurs during the approval stage, which is usually restricted to three to five business days.) I know what you're thinking, but forget it. Killing a deal in this way is perfectly legal in almost all cases.

The Stars of the Show

The only other remaining individuals to discuss are the principals themselves: the buyer and the seller. Suffice it to say, they come in all sizes and shapes and too many different dispositions to list. They range from the shrewd investor who is only concerned about the numbers, to the first-time buyer who is hoping to realize the American Dream. Some sellers are (and I apologize for having to say this) simply big fat jerks. Some buyers are, too. Perhaps it has to do with the intrinsic adversarial nature of the transaction itself. One thing is for certain: A real estate sale seems to bring the worst out in people. Maybe it is because the underlying notion of *caveat emptor* ("Let the buyer beware") gives the impression that the seller is deliberately trying to screw the buyer.

Whatever the reason for it, the tension between buyers and sellers makes real estate an interesting, albeit emotional, way of earning a living for all those in the business in one way or another. I often tell my associates, "Your mission is to keep your head, because in most cases nobody else in the transaction will." Good real estate agents never lose their cool or give way to emotions. It is simply not productive and can only get in the way.

Now that the cast is assembled and we know who is who, we will move on to the next subject: when to buy, when to sell, whom you should listen to, and what questions you need to ask.

Chapter 3

When to Buy, When to Sell

There are two times when it is wise to plant a tree: today and twenty years ago.

—Unknown

f I had a nickel for every time someone came up to me and asked, "So, is this a good time to sell?" I'll bet you I would have . . . an awful lot of nickels. It is without a doubt the number-one-asked question for all real estate brokers.

The flip side to this is question number two: "Is this a good time to buy?" Perhaps this is just a lame attempt at a conversational icebreaker. People asking this question probably really aren't interested in a response; they just want to let someone else take charge of the conversation. I don't let them off so easily, though. My reply is always the same. I move a little closer, and whispering quietly in their ear (so no one else will get the inside track) I say, "That depends." The profundity of this response normally takes them a little aback, and so, right on cue, they ask a little nervously, "It depends on what?" Now they are mine.

Frankly, it depends on too many things to consider. But the most important thing to ask anyone who is looking for the magic answer is, "Are you looking to sell (or buy) right now? If so, what are you looking for, and where are you looking? If you are looking to buy, what is your price range?"

The list goes on and on because the answer to the initial question is totally meaningless unless you get into specifics. Many real estate people love to get into labeling the market in an effort to make themselves sound like authorities. "It's a buyer's market." This may be true for high-end, single-family houses, while not being at all accurate for low-end income-producing property in the same town. It depends on the specifics. To give an appropriate answer, one has to consider what I call *microclimates.*

The area near Buffalo, New York, can serve as a good example of true microclimates in action. Because of the bizarre Lake Erie weather phenomenon known as the Lake Effect, those who live south of the city of Buffalo consistently get dumped with legendary snowfalls. North of the city, on the Niagara Peninsula, they're growing peaches in the summertime. Within a fifty-minute drive south, you're in the western New York wine country. The real estate business is exactly like this in that it includes not just one climate but a series of smaller and very much distinct microclimates.

Thus, the question of whether it is a good time to buy or sell should be posed as follows: "I have a two bedroom duplex, located in such and such, and it is five years old. I bought it new and paid this much for it. If I were to put it on the market tomorrow, what should I expect?" That has narrowed the scope of the market down considerably and now there is room for an intelligent response. The resale market for existing duplexes in this particular part of town could be flooded. It might also be red-hot because there are no resales, a moratorium on new builds for the next year, and there is an incredible consumer demand. Is it a good time to sell? The answer is always much more complex than a simple yes or no.

However, rather than skirt the issue, let me give you some clear-cut guidelines that you need to know in order to start to answer the question better for yourself. At least it will give you a framework to help you adjust your thinking so that you'll know what is important to ask in the first place.

Rule Number One: Follow the Cycle

If you're looking to sell, the following should be your number one rule:

Real estate tends to go in five-year cycles. If there is any chance to gain any kind of appreciation, you can never forget that. Real estate is a type of investment that includes a seasoning period. That's right, you have to start thinking of it like other investments in your portfolio. Like a certificate of deposit, if you sell it too soon there will probably be a serious penalty. But with real estate the situation is actually a little worse. If you sell it too soon, you will run into the problem of being unable to offset your soft costs. What are soft costs? Those are the extra fees that become "the cost of doing business."

"Soft costs" can include marketing the property, brokerage fees, transfer fees, deed stamps, attorney's fees, and so on. In certain cases, your soft costs can run as high as 9 percent of the sale price. Let's say you buy for a hundred, then turn around and try to sell it two years later after the market has had a 5 percent appreciation rate. It may cost you to sell the property simply because of the soft costs.

What if you are selling in an existing subdivision where building is still taking place? You will be at a distinct disadvantage as you will almost always be faced with having to compete with other units that are going *to be built*, which will certainly look more attractive to a new wave of incoming buyers.

The builder, who may be stuck with units he must significantly discount, may be able to sell for less than you paid through special incentives and "sales" that you are unable to match. Also, in most cases he is playing with the bank's money while you are playing with your own.

Another thing to consider if you are asking, "Should I sell now?" is that many people may not want to buy in a half-finished subdivision because of construction inconveniences. Let's face it, if the site is large enough there could be bulldozers and workers kicking up dust for quite some time. Try to sell your existing resale in that environment and you could be facing a long siege, unless you are willing to bite the bullet and take your hit early. Under these circumstances, the answer to the question, "Is it a good time to sell?" could be a more succinct, "No." But again, that depends. You could be in an area of such incredibly high demand it won't make a difference.

It is like asking if commercial versus residential property makes a difference. Absolutely! Existing property versus new construction, as mentioned above, is problematical in any community. Can changes in demographics adversely or positively affect the situation for buying or selling? Most definitely! You must be very careful on this one, however, because if you're not, you could find yourself on the wrong side of federal prosecution due to violations of fair housing regulations. Is the population increasing or decreasing or just shifting to different regions in your area? What is the directional flow? (That is another way of saying, "Where is everyone moving to?") Is there an increase in business activity or jobs that will make an impact on pricing one way or another? Are there substantial political issues that could affect your reason to buy or sell? Examples of this could be disproportionate taxing or the incursion of casino gambling. So as you can see, there are many complicated issues, not including politics, you might first consider when you try to circumvent the five-year rule.

Rule Number Two: Buy and Hold

Here's a fabulous rule of thumb to help answer the question of when you should sell.

Never sell real estate . . . unless you have to sell. Do you remember when you were learning the tricks of the trade concerning multiple-choice tests? In almost all cases, the rule was if you saw the words, "always" and "never" it was probably the wrong answer. However, in this case, it is the correct answer. Don't sell unless you have to. If you don't have to, don't play around on the sale side of the equation. Go play golf instead. It's safer, more enjoyable, and maybe it is even better for your soul.

What would necessitate your having to sell? In the real estate business the vast majority of one's business comes via the DDTs. The what? That's another insider's acronym for *Death, Divorce, and Transfers*. With death, divorce, and transfers (a.k.a. relocation), you pretty much account for all of the "must sell" scenarios that exist. With transfers, we also include the situation of trading up, whereby most people must sell to buy the newer and more expensive home. With death, we have the familiar estate sale where the executor tries to make peace with the family and liquidates the property that has been in the family for forty years. With divorce, usually the wife gets the house. In some cases, however, the courts can force the combatants to sell and split the proceeds. In more amicable divorces (now there's an oxymoron if ever I heard one) the parties simply agree to sell.

Many people like to put their houses on the market at highly inflated prices "just to see if they can get lucky." Sometimes they do, and maybe you could too, but it works so rarely that it really is a thoughtless waste of time. If you hire a broker under such circumstances, it really gets to be perverse. If the broker is unwilling to not talk turkey with you and diplomatically ask, "Are you nuts, or what?" either he is incompetent or cowardly, or else he has a hidden agenda. What could that be, you ask? I'll wager if the broker takes your conspicuously overpriced listing into inventory, he is going to use it to do one of two things:

1. Use the front lawn for incredibly cheap advertising for his company. (That's what the *For Sale* sign is for.)
2. Use your property to help him sell other properties that are better priced by showing yours to be such an incredibly bad value.

So if you are the kind of seller who gets involved with this foolish kind of charade, you deserve all the abuse you'll end up getting. And another thing: Your neighbors will start referring to you as that nut up the street who thinks his house is made of gold.

When should you buy? Simple . . . when you need to buy. "Well, maybe I should just rent," you say. Renting is something you should do only on a very short-term basis. What is short-term? That depends. (I bet you're starting to get the hang of this by now.) Actually, there is a pretty solid answer to this one. Short-term usually means less than eighteen months. Renting for any time longer than that is, in my opinion, the height of fiscal irresponsibility.

I know, I know, you're probably saying, "But I don't have enough money for a down payment." Listen, for at least the last ten years, banks have been practically begging people to borrow money to buy houses. Many states have all sorts of extremely attractive "first-time buyer incentive" programs that are just too attractive to overlook. If you can afford to buy a brand-new car, it is rare that you can't also afford to buy a house, or a condo, a duplex, a co-op, or something.

It's Better to Buy a Cottage Than Rent a Palace

Many readers are probably saying, "Are you kidding? I can't afford to buy in my area." Well, then . . . *move!* Here's another rule for you:

Buy where you can afford to buy and make do until you build your nest egg. It is better to own a hovel than to rent a penthouse. If you don't want to do this and you would rather savor your finely printed rent receipts, then God bless you. But then do yourself a favor and stop reading this book right now! It is a waste of time for you. But wait! Maybe you should hang in there just a tad longer. There may be hope for you yet.

By this point, you may think that I'm being a bit of a wise guy. You might even be thinking, "Who does this guy think he is, talking to us this way?" I'm not going to apologize, though. The Founding Fathers of this country drafted a wonderful document that talked about certain inalienable rights "that among these are Life, Liberty and the Pursuit of Happiness."

This may come as a bit of a shock to you, but Thomas Jefferson stole (excuse me, "borrowed") that phrase from the English philosopher John Locke. In its original version, the phrase was "life, liberty, and property." So important was the concept of property and property ownership that in our earlier days it was a necessity for voting. To my way of thinking, and to Jefferson's, owning property is tantamount to the pursuit of happiness. So if you don't own the place that you are living in, go out and find a way to buy it—or borrow the money from someone else and go out and buy your own piece of the American Dream.

How about investment property? When is the right time to buy? Simple. When the numbers work and you can afford to buy. This is really important, because if the numbers don't work, you really should take a pass and look for another property. Also, you should never feel pressured to buy because it "is the deal of a lifetime." If it is that good, let someone else buy it. You should only look for deals that make sense and are sound investments in the first place. There are many good books on the specific strategies for buying investment properties; you should visit your library and bookstore and read them. Ultimately, you should seek out the best real estate broker you can find and work with him. You should actually wine and dine him because he can help you build your personal fortune like no other professional . . . if you listen to what he has to say and do it.

When to sell? Again, when you have to. Otherwise, hold on forever. When you make the decision to sell your investment property, make sure you structure it as a 1034 Tax Deferred Exchange so you don't relinquish any of your hard-earned profits to capital gains. Check with your broker on this. If he doesn't know about this or is unsure as to the specifics, get another broker. You should also check with your accountant before you attempt to sell any of your investment properties. There could be serious consequences if you don't.

Many times I hear stories about people who could have made more money if they sold at a later date. Some crybaby sellers tell me sob stories about how they lost money selling here or took a bath selling there. To them I say to stop your bellyaching, and remember that real estate is still one of the best investments you can find anywhere. It is also one of the safest. One thing that makes it even better is you can always live in it. Try doing that in a Krugerrand or a hundred shares of Xerox.

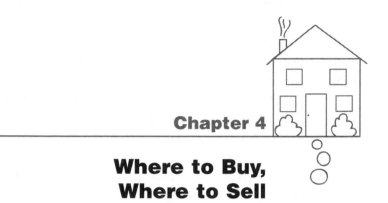

Chapter 4

Where to Buy, Where to Sell

Since there's no other place around the place, this must be the place.

—Lou Costello

've lived in various parts of the United States. It is a great country, a wonderful country. From California to the Gulf Stream waters, ours is a nation of incredible resources and natural beauty. So where is the best place to carve out your own piece of the rock?

You must know the answer by now. *That depends.* If you are a confirmed warm-weather person, there are wonderful opportunities waiting for you in not just the Sun Belt, but all over the Southwest. Many would find it unbelievable, but the number-one place for relocation in the United States through the late '90s was Las Vegas. The Carolinas are also very popular right now, what with the graying of America and with many people getting to an age where the snows of winter are less attractive than they once were.

In general, the overall population is shifting away from the colder, more heavily taxed states of the Northeast. All of this is very interesting, but it may have little to do with you. You see, the important thing to remember is this: Buy where you want to buy. For the time being, forget what the rest of the country is doing and be your own person and follow your own dream.

Now regarding *why* to choose one place over another, that's a different matter entirely. What makes for a hot spot in the first place? There are multitudes of "best lists" around that are worth at least a quick look. But since you are probably a pretty savvy person already (you are reading this book aren't you?), you should look for what is more important than a list. You should seek out readily identifiable patterns to help you determine what's hot and what's, well, not.

Four types of places should emerge as being attractive, or at least "more attractive" than others, with respect to these patterns. The first are those that have some mix of characteristics that make it attractive for certain kinds of companies or other entrepreneurial interests. Why? Because what normally counts first when asking if an area is desirable is business. People need to work, and they will try to live as close to their jobs as possible. Now, granted, there are anomalies. With the advent of the computer and the home business movement, the entire paradigm could change in the next twenty years. An apparent exception to this theory would be the "resort area," but it too is consistent with our model. That's because the resort area's *business* is in fact tourism or leisure itself.

The Best of the Best and the Worst of the Worst

People often ask me where to buy or where they should relocate. There are just so many things to consider when one answers questions like this. Affordability is a major criteria that can help determine a list of best and worst places to live. And to be sure, you can open up a myriad of magazines with all kinds of so-called "best" lists based on every permutation imaginable. Some lists are better than others. *Money* magazine puts out a nifty list and it makes for interesting reading and I have used it to illustrate some interesting points, as you will see later. But will anyone really uproot his or her family and move across the country to go to Rochester, Minnesota, just because right now it ranks pretty far up on the overall list? I think not.

When I started writing this chapter several years ago, I was constantly vexed by the slight changes that would occur on just this one list. What about Atlanta? Atlanta is a pretty hot town right now as well, no pun intended (you do know the locals call it Hotlanta, don't you?).

But I've got to tell you; it is too bloody hot for me, that's for darned sure. Granted, the economy is soaring and so are the planes around their fabulous new airport, but hush my puppies, I don't want to live there either. I hate air conditioning.

One recent list I was perusing recently (Ernst and Young, Kenneth Leventhal Housing Study, 1998) indicated that Raleigh-Durham, North Carolina, was still one of the cheapest places to live, coming in at number 7 on the list. With the incredible growth they have been experiencing in that neck of the woods, I would be hard-pressed to believe that could be true today.

The point is: These lists become outdated almost as quickly as they are printed. Also, everyone's list is different, based on the criteria they select. For me, composite lists are less useful than specific lists, which are more accurate.

Let me see a list that shows cities ranked by median home prices alone. That's useful.

A list showing the crime index is useful. Give me a list that ranks cities by taxes. I could use that, and so could a lot of investors looking to shift a manufacturing plant from one city to another. All that makes sense. Unfortunately, when you start lumping the statistical information together and attempting to develop a list that is supposed to indicate the bests of a series of measurements, you come up with a very questionable list indeed. What the listmakers are trying to demonstrate is that that the closer you are to the top of the list, the closer you are to heaven or that nearly perfect place we all hope to get to someday.

In the end, what you actually get with all these composite lists is a rating system that chambers of commerce use all the time in the hope that they can lure industry and business to their respective areas. Other than that, they serve as much purpose as discussing who wore what to the Oscars. How much time do really informed people spend discussing Blackwell's "worst dressed list" for that matter, either?

From time to time in my real estate practice, I have had the unpleasant job of telling sellers (in buyer's markets) that they may not be able to get the appreciation they might have expected. In seriously soft markets I have had the additionally unpleasant job of informing them that because of *equity erosion* it was highly probable that they would not even break even, and perhaps would have to show up at the closing prepared "to write a check." It was at one such occasion when the seller burst into tears that I heard the question, "Well, where is the best place to buy, then?"

Now before I tell you the answer to that question (or at least how I responded to this client of mine), let's take a look at *Money* magazine's official list for 1997 of what they concluded were the *best* places to live in the U. S. of A. Whether the year is 1997 or 1987 is really not the significant point. What is significant is that they used a specific set of criteria and the list changes from year to year. I'm not saying they're right (or wrong) on this, but this is what they said after an awful lot of figuring. I'm not going to give you all 300 places, just the top twenty. Their decisions were based on a composite of factors, which included: the general economics of the area, arts, commuting time, health services, safety, affordability, climate, and educational standards. Take a look and draw your own conclusions.

Rank City (previous year's rank)

1. Nashua, NH (42)
2. Rochester, MN (3)
3. Monmouth/Ocean Counties, NJ (38)
4. Punta Gorda, FL (2)
5. Portsmouth, NH (44)
6. Manchester, NH (50)
7. Madison, WI (1)
8. San Jose, CA (95)
9. Jacksonville, FL (20)
10. Fort Walton Beach, FL (18)
11. Seattle, WA (36)
12. Gainesville, FL (18)
13. San Francisco, CA (68)
14. Lakeland, FL (10)
15. Fort Lauderdale, FL (4)
16. Raleigh/Durham/Chapel Hill, NC (24)
17. West Palm Beach, FL (25)
18. Orlando, FL (12)
19. Boulder, CO (28)
20. Long Island, NY (90)

Notice anything? Well at first glance these places seem like they're all over the board. In some cases you might even say quietly to yourself, "God, I wouldn't get caught dead in that place." In some cases I would agree with that, too. But a closer look shows a definite trend. It also shows that real estate is dynamic and nothing stays the same. There was considerable movement in positions from one year to the next.

Do you see the pattern now? Of the top twenty, eight are in Florida. That's 40 percent of the total. If you want to ask how many of these are in warmer climates (the drift toward the Sun Belt), add three more and you have better than half. Let's think about that for a moment. Now I like Florida. I know a lot of people live there and a lot of people want to move there, many of whom are not collecting Social Security. But for me at least, and who knows, maybe some of you might even agree with me, *it's hotter than blazes in Florida in the summertime!* What can I tell you, I am one of those guys who enjoys a change of seasons.

And I love San Francisco. I just can't afford to live there (the number-one most expensive place to live). Remember *Money's* best list was made up of a series of factors, each of which was averaged to make a final determination. Long Island is a pretty neat place, it made it to the top twenty, and heck, I even lived there for twenty-odd years myself. But try commuting when you live there. It is simply awful.

Money magazine quite deferentially declined to issue an official top list in 2001 in the wake of 9/11. They chose to recognize NYC as the coolest place to be and I applaud them for saluting my hometown. But just to give some balanced reporting on how the list would appear if we made it more current, I compiled an unofficial list using the same criteria they used to complete the previous list. It pretty much looks the same. But in my updated list little old Pittsburgh shows up at #8. Now a lot of people out there who have never been to Pittsburgh might say, "Hey, they don't call it Pitts for nothing." Obviously, they don't know what they are talking about. It's a great city. Except for all the one-way streets that serve to confuse anyone who isn't a native, it is difficult to not love Pittsburgh. Stack it up against Buffalo (#137) and there are lots of similarities. The numbers of sunny days are about the same. Vehicle insurance and cost of living are also quite similar. The big differences are snowfall, taxes, and the job index.

Now back to the poor lady who asked me through her tears, "Well, where is the best place to buy?" The answer I gave her then still stands: "Wherever you can find happiness." You may have just rolled your eyes, but it's true. I proved it the very next day. At my sales meeting (I was working in Orchard Park, New York, a suburb of Buffalo),

I asked how many of my associates liked living where they were living. They all said they did. I reminded them that Buffalo/Niagara Falls came out very poorly at #228 (1997) on the list of desirable places to live. There were so many other *better* places, at least according to *Money*.

To illustrate my point I had them participate in the following exercise. I invited them all to take an imaginary bus trip, which was going to be a tour of places to live. The rules of the game were that they could live anywhere they liked. I stopped at the first ten places on the list. Only one person got off the bus. Where do you think she decided to get off? That's right. She gracefully disembarked at Punta Gorda, Florida. She said she had relatives there and it was very nice.

Hopefully, I've made my point. So many places have a lot going for them that lists like this are interesting, but will they really have you packing your bags and ordering up the U-Haul? Probably not, I think. The truth is that there are great things to be said about lots of places. You just need to find yours. You have to find your own happiness and a place you select off a list to move to may not have a lot to do with it.

Chapter 5

"FSBO or Not FSBO . . . That Is the Question"

—Hamlet, on selling his first castle in Denmark

ere's the chapter you may have been waiting for if you are an eager seller hoping to save yourself some money. For the uninitiated, the term "FSBO" is an acronym that means *For Sale By Owner*. There are many reasons why people elect to go it alone when deciding to sell their own house, but there are only two reasons that are worth any consideration. One, the seller thinks they will save themselves a commission, and two, they just don't like real estate agents. That's it in a nutshell.

Before we get to the pros and cons of the FSBO decision for sellers (one that can adversely effect a seller's equity position), let me say one thing to any purchaser considering buying a house directly from an owner. *Don't do it!* In virtually all cases you will overpay for the property. You'll see why in a moment.

Periodically, I try to get my salespeople to consider why their clients and customers need them. The question I pose at a sales meeting isn't about what kind of a good job you can do for the typical seller. It is this: "How many of you out there have ever tried to install a toilet on you own?" (Like any good lawyer, I like to ask questions where I have a reasonable shot at knowing how my witness will answer.) More often than not, most of my audience will answer in the negative. On one occasion, one woman raised her hand. I couldn't believe it. There she sat, dressed to the nines, with fingernails that could be declared lethal weapons, and she said smugly, "I have. I have installed a toilet."

I hate it when I have an audience in the palm of my hand and somebody just won't cooperate. So I tried a different tactic and asked her, "But would you do it again?"

"Hell, no," she barked back.

"Why not," I asked? She looked at me smiling and exclaimed, "Because it's a pain in the neck, and I don't have the time for it, and if I want it done now, and I want it done right, I'll call a plumber."

That's exactly the point! Selling a house on your own is a pain in the butt, too. That's why real estate agents get paid a lot of money to do it. Remember this: In virtually all cases when agents take you on as a client, they do so on a contingency basis. If they don't succeed, you owe them nothing, nada, zip. It's their risk, their time, and their money invested.

Still, if you are the headstrong type and you want to sell your own house, you should at least know what your odds are. The National Association of Realtors estimates that sellers successfully sell their houses (without the help of a professional) in fewer than one in five of the transfers. A full 81 percent of all of the homes on the market are sold with the guidance of an agent in the business.

For those people who fall into the other 19 percent and succeed, my hat is off to them. I'm willing to guess, though I can't prove it, that in 95 percent of those cases the seller at one point or another in the transaction yelled the word, *"Heeeeeelp!"* But I know based on selling and managing the sales of well over a billion dollars worth of real estate that agents themselves yell that all the time—and they're in the business and know what they're doing.

Selling a home is kind of like running the steeplechase in the Olympics. You have to be well prepared, know what you're doing, and recognize that you will have to get over or around an awful lot of obstacles. So here's what you need to know if you want to run the course yourself. There are at least twenty-four obstacles before you get to the finish line. On your mark, get set, go!

Obstacle #1: The Myth of the Saved Commission

Simply put, this is the biggest myth when you try to sell your house on your own. Do you really think that the buyer is stupid? To the contrary, buyers are quite savvy today. With FSBO houses they believe, justified or not, that: (a) the owner overpriced the house, and (b) that what the owner really hopes to get is a price that is inflated by the amount of the commission. In this way, if he can't sell the house and has to turn it over to a broker, he can afford to discount it by 6 to 7 percent at that point.

Assuming that the buyer thinks this way, he will automatically negotiate you down to the lower price right out of the box. It goes something like this: "You want a hundred? I'll give you ninety-three. After all, that's what you would have netted if you were working with a broker, right?" Whether the seller pays for the commission or not, it's still considered to be part of the deal.

Obstacle #2: Pricing—Too Much or Too Little

If you are a layman, and "not in the business," you cannot possibly have a firm grip on exactly what price you should ask for the house. One of the hardest things the broker has to accomplish is to get the house priced so that it sells in a time period that is consistent with current market conditions. Real estate is constantly changing and it takes a lot of skill (and years of experience) to learn how to read a market so that the seller is maximizing his chance of making a deal that is deemed fair to all parties.

Many sellers think they can put any price on a property and see what happens. Usually, in situations like this, *nothing* happens. I call this the "sucker" theory. "There has to be one out there and I am going to wait until he comes along." Guess who the sucker usually winds up being? Anyone have a mirror?

Obstacle #3: Qualifying Potential Buyers

Again, unless you are in the real estate or mortgage financing business, you run the risk of getting lucky and snagging a buyer, and then finding out he may not be qualified to finance the purchase. "That's his problem," you may say. Nope—if he can't get a mortgage, and his deal falls through, you could incur legal expenses that greatly offset any commissions you might have saved, not to mention time lost on the market. As an extra negative, do you think the house will sell for more the second time around? I'll bet you a buck it doesn't. No matter where you live, if you think your neighbors don't know that your deal fell through, you'd better think again.

Obstacle #4: The "I'm Just Looking" Crowd

Neighbors want to look. Every Tom, Dick, and Sidney wants to look. Those homeowner ads smoke out "lookers" like you wouldn't believe. Ninety-five percent of those looking probably don't have two nickels to rub together and certainly can't afford your home. Brokers are supposed to prequalify all those lookers to determine if they have the necessary gelt should they actually want to buy. Try asking those guys who just rode up on the Harleys, "Say, are you sure you can afford this luxury three-bedroom domicile, or are you wasting my time just as I was getting ready to serve afternoon tea?"

Obstacle #5: Henry Kissinger, You're Not

Are you going to do your own negotiations? This is where many brokers really shine. Call it the art of the deal, but really good agents start to salivate once they get to this part of the process. When you try to negotiate for yourself, you can forget the Don Corleone school of real estate ("It's not personal, it's business"). If you're negotiating for yourself, it's entirely personal.

There is no way you can separate yourself. If you think you can, you are delusional. In the legal world they say, "A lawyer who handles his own case has a fool for a client." When Richard Nixon got into trouble, he hired an attorney. This was a man who was not only the president, but also an expert trial lawyer. It is the same way in real estate. You are probably better off letting someone else do it.

Obstacle #6: The Hidden Objection

Because it seems too personal, prospects are often reluctant to express their objections directly to the owner. Nobody wants to hurt anybody's feelings. Having an intermediary can help smoke out those smaller objections so you can move on to the more significant points. An agent might say, "You don't like the wallpaper? Fine, how much would it really cost you to change it? Let's get back to what you really like about the house." This was in response to the statement, "God, what idiot picked out that red flocked wallpaper? I've never seen anything so horrid!" The customer would never say such a thing out loud to you, who might have spent hours searching through wallpaper pattern books to find that very choice.

Obstacle #7: Learning to Handle Objections Big and Small

A big part of a good agent's training goes into handling all sorts of serious, as well as not so serious, objections. An experienced agent has already dealt with all the reasons buyers have for deciding not to buy, or for changing their minds after they have decided to buy. What may appear as a crisis confrontation to you should be business as usual for a sharp agent. If you're not up to the game, a sale could be lost.

Obstacle #8: The Urgency Factor

If your time to sell is short, you cannot afford to try it on your own. Statistically we have already told you that under the best of circumstances the odds are decidedly against you. If you blow it, you have lost your narrow window of opportunity. Will moving out and leaving your house vacant enhance your bargaining position? I don't think so. Also, if you take your chances and lose, the broker has had his bargaining position somewhat eroded as well. He is getting a house that sat on the market for weeks and months with nothing happening.

Obstacle #9: Financing Problems

This goes beyond the qualifying problems of obstacle #3. Let's presume the buyers have their financing in place and something goes screwy at the bank. Do you have the expertise to be able to pull some strings? (Legally, of course.) Will you have the vision or the aptitude to direct the purchaser to another bank if necessary? Will you be able to save the deal when it starts to flounder because of some bureaucratic foul-up at the bank? Will you know when the buyer is telling you the truth about the actual status of the missing letter of commitment?

Brokers do business all the time with scores of different banks. They have established relationships that are important to them as well as to the banks. Don't underestimate the importance of a broker's role just on this one point alone. It could save your deal.

Obstacle #10: You Lack Prospect Sources

The more exposure a home has to more qualified buyers the quicker it will sell. In reality, most homeowners are limited in their sources of prospects—friends, relatives, bulletin boards, local advertising, and the Internet.

By contrast, any successful broker has a huge and constantly renewing flow of prospects from all of these sources. In addition, he will have relocation assistance and a broker network that the FSBO does not have immediate access to. The homeowner acting alone has a clear and nearly insurmountable obstacle with #10.

Obstacle #11: Limited Advertising Exposure

The owner gets to advertise one house—his own. Unfortunately, people buy based on comparisons. Here the broker shines once again, because he has many homes to show and advertise. He has a great assortment of wares on his shelves. Incidentally, it is rare indeed that a would-be homebuyer purchases the first house they look at. In addition, brokers know something that the average homeowner may not know. Advertising doesn't sell homes. It only serves to help build traffic to provide an ambiance so that the purchaser is more inclined to choose.

Obstacle #12: The Follow-up System

Rarely does a house get sold at first sight. A sale usually emerges after a second, third, or more visits. The broker usually has a follow-up system of customers who haven't yet purchased. Also the broker representative will accompany prospects on inspections of other properties and when the appropriate buy signal is made they will bring them back to your home in an effort to close the sale. You can't do that when you are on your own.

It is also very common for shoppers at open houses to give phony names to sellers. This happens to professionals, too. The seasoned pro, however, is used to sniffing out the live ones and acting when the time is right. They can also follow up with them a lot better than you can.

Obstacle #13: The Contingent Sale

One of the most difficult sales to make is also one of the most common: the contingent sale. This refers to the big contingency, the sale of one house to purchase another.

This is as tricky a game plan for the professional as you can imagine. It is so difficult that some markets do not allow them and some relocation firms will not even consider an offer that is contingent. How can the homeowner even begin to decide how viable the sale is? Making this determination is based solely on information and knowledge concerning the salability of the backup house. This information may not be accessible to the homeowner.

Here are some questions that need to be asked:

1. Is the "backup" house on the market?
2. Is it on with a broker or do we have one FSBO backing up another FSBO? Talk about long shots!
3. How long has it been on the market?
4. How many showings has it had?
5. How many offers has it had?
6. If it has had offers, what were they, and why weren't they accepted?
7. What is the turnover rate of houses in that area? What is the price range?
8. Is the agent working on that sale, full time or part-time? What is his track record?
9. How much equity will they derive from that sale, and will it be enough to purchase your house? Remember, they have now doubled their closing costs.
10. How are you going to ask these very pertinent and invasive questions of strangers? The broker can do that because it's nothing personal, it's business.

Obstacle #14: The Owner Assumes the Expenses

If you try to sell on your own you have to assume all the financial burdens of advertising at open rates, signage, and marketing the home. It's true that these expenses will amount to considerably less than a sales commission if you are successful. When you fail, however, you will have to tack these expenses on to the cost of the commission you will be charged by the broker, thus further eating into your equity.

Obstacle #15: Sales Is a Business, Not a Hobby

Selling houses is a business. That's just the way it is. In addition to knowing about the art of selling (i.e., closing, handling objections, asking for the order, etc.), one has to take into consideration the curious nature of selling homes. There is no commodity more emotional than the place where a person lives. Special training and skills are needed here, and they don't necessarily translate if you are used to selling widgets or waffle irons. The FSBO has a clear disadvantage here.

Obstacle #16: The Buyer's Reluctance to Really Inspect

Most buyers feel ill at ease poking around your cupboards and closets with you standing there over them. Tell me you're not standing there over them. Sure you are. You want to make sure that they don't miss a detail. Naturally they clam up and say things like, "Oh, this is nice, how lovely." They really don't tell you what they think. With an agent present, and you conspicuously absent, buyers shoot right out with comments like, "Yeah, those coffee-colored countertops are the first thing we'd change." The agent recognizes these as buy signals, not as criticisms. You might be horrified, but such comments provide an atmosphere for the agent to get further agreement on all the other things they do like about the property.

Obstacle #17: Justifying the Sale Price

This is near to impossible for the FSBO. First of all, they can't help it, but they are just too damned subjective about the whole price issue. Many times agents laugh at the prices that sellers come up with and the rationale that they have used to set the price. Often times, homeowners will give themselves an appreciation rate that is beyond ludicrous, as though appreciation is something one should just tack on. The appreciation in an area is something that professionals track constantly, and it literally changes with the seasons, not just the year. Sometimes you have depreciation. Rarely have I seen a FSBO admit that it is even possible that his or her house might have dropped in value. This is sometimes a difficult concept even after the house has sat on the market for years with no activity. "It's not the price," they say, "it's that people don't understand what I've put into this house." Floyd Wickman, a nationally famous real estate sales trainer, refers to this as the heavy-duty nail syndrome. Frankly, nobody is going to care (or pay) for the platinum-laced nails you've used.

Sellers will often base the sale price on what they paid, plus a mythological appreciation rate, plus what they put into it. Many times expenditures added were maintenance items like a new roof or a hot water heater. Yes, they cost a lot of money. But most sellers are shocked when they learn that most buyers today just expect to get a roof on the house, hot water isn't considered to be a luxury extra, and a buyer is not going to pay you more for them.

Agents come up with a price by sifting through comparable sales and factors of supply and demand and come up with a very cold competitive market analysis. This shows what the house will sell for without all the subjective nonsense that the seller thinks is important. Remember, the seller isn't buying the house. The buyer is.

Obstacle #18: Hello, Is Anyone Home?

Unless you have decided to make yourself a prisoner in your own house, you are going to lose showings. Buyers don't want to look at your house when it is convenient for you. They want to look at it now. Selling a house is not supposed to be something that is convenient. Sellers really cut their own throats on this one. In fact, many times sellers will list their homes with one of my agents and then make a series of demands and stipulations on when they can show the property. "We need forty-eight hours' notice . . . We will allow showings only on weekends prior to 5:00 P.M. . . . You can show the house only during cycles of the full moon and when the sky is 60 percent cloud-covered."

Hello! Are you kidding? Many times I will tell the agent to terminate the listing agreement and go and find a seller who wants to sell for real. I always tell sellers upfront, "We will try to minimize your inconvenience, but recognize this will be, at times, an inconvenience."

That's because selling a home and living in it are two different things. And, frankly, selling a home can be a royal pain in the butt. Buyers will traipse through your home and say the stupidest and rudest things you can imagine. (Try not to listen, or better yet, try not to be around for those remarks. It's tough enough to uproot yourself without having to listen to dumb comments.)

Obstacle #19: Strangers in the Night

When you put the *For Sale* sign up in your yard, it is an open invitation for every nut in town to walk up and say, "Hey, can I look at your house?" Added to this is the issue of fair housing. If you don't like the way someone looks, or if you think someone has come at an inappropriate time, you could have more problems than the obvious ones. You could be looking at issues of discrimination because of your implied screening of the property. Wow, now you have the federal government on your case. I often wonder what the average guy says when the scary biker brigade shows up wanting to see the house. "Excuse me, but could you come back on the weekend when the little woman is at home?" Oh boy. Wouldn't you rather have a broker, legally, safely, and quietly do the screening for you and make sure that anyone looking at your house is qualified and prescreened?

Obstacle #20: People Judge a Book by Its Cover

How do you get buyers to come "inside" when all they do is drive by the "outside" and say, "too small . . . I don't like the color, etc." I really get a charge out of those sign riders that say *"must see inside."* Sharp real estate agents know how to entice lookers and passersby to get out of their cars to take a good look inside. They don't do it with those silly sign riders either. Unless you are going to block traffic and commandeer the cars as they drive by, I don't know how you are going to force people to look inside your house.

Obstacle #21: You're Out of Here

Here's a great reason to never buy a house directly from a homeowner. After the sale is closed the seller is gone, *outta here.* Generally, there is no future contact and that's just fine in most cases. If there is an agent involved and something goes wrong just after settlement, there is some recourse or possible remedy. The agent wants to make things right. He has a reputation and could be looking for future business. Agents are under legal constraints to tell the truth and treat all parties fairly for which they can suffer monetary and other more serious consequences if they slip up. The seller can simply shrug his shoulders and say, "Hey, *caveat emptor,* buddy . . . don't bother me."

Obstacle #22: Who Are You Going to Believe?

Many people find it hard to accept everything that a real estate agent says as being the Gospel truth. They presume that the agent wants to make a sale and they're right. As such, they further conclude that the agent might be given to certain exaggerations, or to what is known in the business of selling as "seller's puff." The agent definitely has an interest in getting the house sold. There is no question there. But what about the seller himself, you ask? If buyers take what agents have to say with a grain of salt, what are they taking with the seller himself, a whole salt block? Both the agent and the seller clearly have a problem in the credibility department. The agent does have an edge, however, because his livelihood is threatened if he is found to do more than just puffing and is, in fact, misrepresenting the property. The importance of one property isn't worth telling falsehoods when stacked up against reputation and future business.

Obstacle #23: Getting It Closed

Once the sale is made, a complicated process commences, which leads to the final resolution of the transaction. In some parts of the country it is simply called the *closing*. In others they call the *settlement process*. The terms are really interchangeable. Agents laugh all the time when sellers think that all they get paid for is to find a buyer. Here's a point to consider: In most states the commission is deemed earned when there is a meeting of the minds. When an agent finds a buyer who is ready, willing, and able to buy, his job from a legal sense in over.

If you are a seller, you should always make payment due and payable only upon the successful closing of the property. This should be written directly into the listing agreement. Usually it can be placed in the "remarks section of the contract." This insulates you from having to pay a commission if the transaction dies—but back to our obstacle here. Getting the property closed is like throwing a touchdown pass when it's third down and long. Agents have a tough time quarterbacking the transaction from contract to closing, but that's their job. They are well versed in whom to call at the bank, how to talk to an appraiser, and how to smooth over the feathers of the buyer when he or she gets nuts—as they most likely will at some point. The FSBO seller really falls short of resolving this hurdle effectively, unless he is in the business himself or has bought and sold scores of properties in the market in which they are currently trying to sell.

It's not just about making the sale. It is getting it closed that really counts. Agents need to really focus their energies to get properties to close. So much work is done behind the scenes after the contract is executed that I sometimes think that they should charge a separate fee for these services. Unless the FSBO wants to make this his full-time job, he is putting himself at considerable risk in not having the property close on time if he tries to do it himself.

Obstacle #24: This Old House

That's the name of a popular television program. It also refers to a very common query when a buyer makes the earliest buy signal. "How long has this house been on the market?" Every buyer asks this. With fruits and vegetables, if they have been around for a long time, there is spoilage. With a house there is a reduction of value. Buyers are especially tuned into this if they are buying in the area they are currently living in and not relocating from the outside. If the seller fails to sell it on his own and subsequently lists the house with a broker, valuable marketing time is lost. Worse still, the question comes up again. Only this time it is phrased like this: "Hasn't this house been on the market forever. I remember seeing the owner trying to sell it on his own. I guess he gave up and came to his senses. How much did you say he wanted?"

Here's a quick rule of thumb. If a house hasn't sold in a reasonable period of time it was probably overpriced in the first place. What's a reasonable period? That depends on your particular market. In very solid seller's markets, the answer might be a month. In parts of the Midwest, it could be six months. Brokers know what is reasonable. Civilians rarely have an accurate read on this, unless they fully immerse themselves in serious research and have access to a comprehensive database of recent closings in their area.

When it ultimately sells after a longer period (and the following is an almost infallible rule), the property will sell for less than what it would have sold for if it was properly priced in the first place. "Market age" is one of the most common causes of equity erosion and loss of value. Price it right. Give it to a broker, to get the job done right.

Those are the twenty-four obstacles or hurdles you are going to have to overcome if you are to get to the finish line and get your house sold. If it sounds like I am being less than encouraging about FSBO and that I am advocating the use of a broker, you're right. At the sales meeting I described at the beginning of this chapter, I asked how many had installed a toilet. Selling your own house is not very different in this way: You certainly *can* do it, but it's just not that easy. It makes sense that I should at least warn you of what to expect.

If after reading this chapter you still want to try it on your own, hey, knock yourself out. It's a free country and everyone has a right to do things that aren't necessarily in their best interests. But if you are going to be persistent, let me give you a few pointers.

You've got the hurdles in front of you. You know what they are. Here are the key issues: Value in real estate is comprised of three factors: price, location, and condition. Unless you can put the house on wheels, forget about location. You're stuck with that. The condition is something that is within your power to adjust. Get the property as shipshape and presentable as soon as you can. It has to be top-notch to get top dollar.

Above all else, get it priced right. How do you do that? You could call three brokers and get them to do a market analysis and then just forget to hire any of them after you've picked their brains. That is a very weenie-like thing to do, however. No, if you want to do it alone, do it alone. You could pay someone to come in and do an independent fee appraisal. It's kosher to do that. But using professionals and trying to slide by without paying them is just a very uncool thing to do and invites a big payback on the wheel of karma.

After you have your "paid for" appraisal, take that price and see how it compares with other properties currently being offered for sale in your area. Price yourself 5 percent under the closest comparable property and you have a good shot at overcoming most of those obstacles we talked about in this chapter.

Another key point is building traffic. Some brokers offer a menu of services on a fee basis. If you have access to a broker who will give you multiple listing services for less than a full commission, you can probably beat the odds and get your house sold. You still have to be priced right, however. The market will be relentless on this point. With multiple listing services available to you, you will be getting a good amount of cooperation from the brokerage community. They will figure that in cases like these 50 percent of a fee is better than no fee if yours is the perfect house for their customer. What if this kind of fee for service is not available? Here's another way to tackle this issue.

There are various agency relationships you can elect to enter into when working with a broker. If you are still hellbent on doing it on your own, consider the following. Opt for an exclusive agency relationship rather than an exclusive right to sell. The former allows you to sell it on you own and pay no commission. The latter does not. If you can get the exclusive agency relationship, you have, in effect, hedged your bets. If the broker finds a buyer you pay a commission. If you get lucky and after having the property exposed to the market through the broker, you stumble across a buyer at a cocktail party on your own, congratulations you win and you don't have to pay.

So that's it on doing it the hard way. People try to do it all the time. Some actually succeed and you can, too. But remember, it will be the hardest work you have ever done and in the end only you will be able to determine if it was worth it. Remember the agent who said she had installed her own toilet? She wouldn't do it again. She'd call a plumber. You might want to call a Realtor, or better still have a friend recommend a good one for you.

Chapter 6

Buying and Selling
Success Guaranteed

I made my money by selling too soon.
—Bernard Baruch

How much time do you have available to spend navigating the flow charts of real estate investing? Not much? No problem, because I am going to make this very simple. We will limit our scope to residential property simply because there are too many other books on the subject that will delve a lot deeper into financial analysis than we can here.

Success means different things to different people. I was recently showing a very nice property to a young couple and they asked me if I thought the house was a good buy. My response may have seemed somewhat philosophical to them because I answered by saying, "Yes, it is an excellent buy. If you buy it and live here happily, how could it not be?" Marcus Aurelius, the great Roman emperor, said it so much better than me when he noted that, "Even in a palace a man might live well." I see so many people buying and selling homes, trading up, trading down, making money, losing money, shattering their family's lives in the process, and thinking that they are being shrewd real estate investors.

I know one individual who has moved no less than fourteen times, scrupulously trading up and building a little equity each time. He currently lives in one of the finest subdivisions in my area. To an outside observer, he has been the shrewdest of the shrewd and often tells his success story to anyone who is willing to listen. His quest for wealth, or more precisely "building wealth" by buying and trading real estate, is relentless. He tells his tale by explaining that, "Real estate is not unlike any other investment and as such I expect to get a better return on my investment than I would, say, in the stock market. Real estate is not a place to live so much as it is a commodity to be traded. And each time I make the trade, hopefully, I sell for more than I paid."

Financially, my friend has done very well following this plan and you can, too. The only point I would make is that in this particular person's case, he bought and sold a great many houses, but in the twenty or so years he spent doing this, he never once bought a home. The return he realized personally was that he got to live in the "house of strangers" many times over. I would rate his success as very low. Others might view the same facts and rate his performance very high. It all goes back to the all-important issue: "How do we define success?"

An overall definition of success should include that we get a reasonable return on our financial outlay. Certainly, we should not lose money. More important, however, is that we base our decision to buy or sell on how it will affect the quality of our lives. Sometimes money is not the best indicator. The following are some points to ponder.

Rules of the (Real Estate) Road

With respect to selling, that's easy. Here's the simple rule I mentioned before: You only sell when you have to sell. I also touched on the three must-sell situations referred to in the real estate business as the DDTs: death, divorce, and transfer. With death, usually the estate will sell off the property. However, if the family is well off and somehow able to keep the property in the family without it causing a financial burden, I would maintain that the property should not be sold. Investments like real estate tend to be very secure in terms of holding value. Unless the home is in an area where property values are noticeably declining, it still might make sense to hang on to it unless practical matters, like who is going to provide for the upkeep, become an issue.

Divorce is another typical must-sell scenario, although it doesn't always have to be. If either side can see his or her way clear to buy the other party out, the property should, in most cases, remain with one person or the other. Sometimes the reasons for selling are not purely economic. The wife may say that she simply has to "get on with her life." So be it. That is a decision based on a choice, not a must-sell situation.

Transfer usually spells SELL. If you need to buy in a different state and you must pull your equity out of the house you currently live in to do so, we are talking a must-sell scenario. Again, if the person moving is well-heeled enough to buy without selling, there could be an opportunity for some serious wealth building. The house that is being moved out of could become a nice income property if the owner is able to rent it out, thus providing a positive cash flow.

Of course, the owners could be missing out on some serious tax sheltering based on capital gains rules. Under code 1054 of the IRS tax regulations, all of the capital gains on a primary residence can be deferred indefinitely provided the house you are buying exceeds the taxable base on the house you are selling. Currently, you have two years to roll over your equity together with your appreciation and whatever gain may have been realized from the sale. The key here is determining your cost basis. Here's an example.

Original purchase price:	$50,000
Miscellaneous improvements:	+ $25,000
Soft costs (commissions, marketing, etc.):	+ $5,250
Cost basis:	$80,250

As a general rule, those are your must-sell scenarios. If you can at all see yourself clear to hold on, you should. On the other hand, quality of life issues do come into play. What if you have bought several properties and now the neighborhoods have started to change and become unsafe? You are now nervous about rent collection and being able to maintain the properties. One solution might be to enlist the aid of a property manager. If after building their fee into the operating expense it still makes financial sense to hang on, again, you should do so. But if you are tired of the hassle, you don't want to look for property managers, and you just want out, you should sell even if it has a negative impact on you financially. If the reward of the removal of the burden outweighs the problems of holding onto the property, then you should sell.

From time to time I hear sellers say, "I just want out, I just want to dump it. It doesn't really matter what I get out of the sale, just get rid of it." This leads to another handy-dandy rule of thumb: The stronger the motivation to sell, the better the buying opportunity. If you're a buyer, look for those with strong motivation to sell. Agents are always looking for their most motivated sellers. This helps those agents turn their inventory, and earn a living. Words that make an agent shudder when they speak to a possible seller are, "I'm really in no hurry to sell, if I get my price that's fine, otherwise I can wait." Guess what—agents can't afford to wait. They shouldn't bother to either, not if they are in the business of selling real estate, as opposed to merely taking listings.

Beyond the DDTs: Tips for When and How to Sell

Here's another tip on selling, or when not to sell: *Never break the five-year rule.* Real estate is a cyclical business and generally goes in five-year cycles. If you buy a house and try to sell it in a year or two, unless you're in an area of tremendous appreciation (15 percent or more) you will almost always get hurt. Let's consider the following scenario. Suppose you are in an area where homes are appreciating at about 3 percent per year. You try to sell in two years. Your closing costs alone will be greater than your appreciation, and you could come out netting a negative return. Let's plug in some numbers.

Purchase price:	$200,000
Two years' appreciation at 3%:	+ 12,000
Current value:	$212,000
Closing costs (estimated at 8%):	− $16,960
Return from sale:	$195,040

Based on this example, with this appreciation rate and estimated closing costs (conservatively projected at 8 percent; realistically, it would probably be 9 percent or more), you come out close to five grand in the hole. It would take a minimum of three years to get back on the plus side, so you can see why a five-year holding period makes more sense.

Here's another tip: *When you make the decision to sell, get your price to rock bottom as fast as you can.* The longer you hold out, the less you will realize when you ultimately sell. This means whether you choose to use a Realtor or not, price yourself so competitively that your house must sell before the competition does. If the other guys want to hold out, let them. Here's something I'll bet you didn't know. Generally speaking, your first offer is your best. All good agents know this. If your first offer comes in significantly lower than your asking price, chances are you are asking way too much—which leads me to the next tip.

Always be willing to negotiate. When the market in my area went soft, I started instructing my agents to prep all their sellers to remember that when they had an offer come in, there were only two choices. They could accept or counter. A "No" response is not part of what I would call a negotiation.

The typical modus operandi of many sellers when a low-ball offer is tendered is to act insulted. I understand that reaction in a tough-guy kind of way, but to such sellers my only advice is, "Grow up!" An offer is insulting? Insulting is when an agent comes to you and says something disparaging about your mother. Insulting is not when he tells you someone is very much interested in buying your home and they want to discuss the terms and price of the purchase.

When what is perceived as an unrealistically low offer is placed, the offer should always be countered (unless it is accepted). Let me repeat that word for emphasis: *always.* The counteroffer may not be significant, but it has to give the purchaser the indication that there is some movement toward a meeting of the minds. I discussed earlier in this book the concept of the five P's that must be dealt with in any successful agreement: the *parties*, the *payment*, the *property*, *possession*, and the *price*. If you have agreement on three or four of five, and price is the sticking point, then work with it.

Let's say the price is $200,000. (By the way, that is the actual price, not the *asking price*. Whenever the word "asking" is placed in front of the word "price," it means that the seller or the seller's agent don't imagine even in their wildest dreams that anyone is going to be silly enough to give them anything close to that number.) The price is $200,000. The offer is $130,000. That is too big a gap for the seller to say that the buyer is serious, right? Wrong. If the seller wants to get somewhere in the high 180s to low 190s, he shouldn't say, "No, go home." A reasonable counter might be $194,000. The purchaser laughs, and says, "What, are you kidding?" The purchaser then offers $145,000. The seller moves to $190,000.

The purchaser ups his bid to $165,000. The seller declares "No deal," and gives a final counteroffer of $187,000. The purchaser comes back with $175,000. Now if the negotiation has reached a stalemate, I am willing to speculate that the property is probably worth somewhere between $175,000 and $187,000. If the seller was working with me, I would tell him to pray these folks come back. I would tell him that some number over $175,000 is the right number for this house (I would further wager that my study of comparable houses would support this). Any offer in the 180s is one that the seller should take and run like the wind with. Granted, his original expectations were much higher. But so many times expectations are a far cry from reality. What would have happened if the seller did like most people and refused to counter this ridiculously low initial offer? Nothing, which is why I constantly quote Einstein, "Nothing occurs in the universe without movement." Move. Learn to work with people, whatever they come to you with, before you stonewall.

Tips for Sellers

Tip #1: *Sellers should always work with a good real estate attorney.*

That's the first tip (more of a rule, actually) for sellers. Buyers should too, but it is even more crucial for the seller because he is the one conveying the property. There is more to screw up on the sell side of the equation. And don't be afraid to fire your attorney if you feel he or she is not getting you to the goal line. You want an attorney who is not afraid to flex his legal muscles if the buyer starts to get squirrelly. This is not the forum for wimpy lawyers. Those without savvy need not apply. A wimpy attorney can add months of anguish and too many dollars to his fee while he fumbles around with your deal. Get somebody with teeth. It will end up being a lot cheaper in the long run. Again, all of this advice holds true for the buyer as well. I just emphasize it more strongly for the seller.

Tip #2: *When negotiations bog down, always reduce it to a dollars-and-cents issue.*

When the buyer starts flipping out over the fireplace utensils, reduce it to a dollar amount and ask yourself, do I really need to blow a deal for $50 to $100? If you think about it that way, it probably isn't worth arguing over. Bear in mind, however, that if the pattern has been established that the buyer is going to nickel and dime you to death and the contract still hasn't been executed, you may want to pass and get a more mature buyer.

Tip #3: *If the buyer wants a home inspection, God bless him, let him have one.*

Keep two things in mind, though: The seller should never pay for it. *Never.* If the buyer wants a home inspection, terrific, just make sure he pays for it.

Also, have the buyer do his home inspection before he puts in his offer. Many buyers and their agents will balk at this. They will say, "Well, yes, but I want to tie the property up while I am deciding whether or not I should buy." To this I always respond, "Sorry about that. If you want a home inspection, that's fine. It will make us both feel better that you are getting just the house you want. You will get a clear fix in your own mind about what deferred maintenance you can expect in the next five years or so. Just don't try to tie me up in the process." More to the point, if the buyer buys your house subject to a home inspection, I'll bet you that your chances are better than even that he tries to come back and renegotiate the deal. This is very frustrating and sets an even worse tone for the transaction. If he does his inspection before the offer, you'll only get hammered on your price once, not twice.

Tip #4: *Keep any contingencies to the sale under control.*

Accept them or don't accept them, that's your call. But, if you do elect to sell your house subject to the sale of another house, make sure the house is on the market with a reputable broker and that it is priced right, etc. No FSBOs here. Also, offers with contingencies frequently have "call" provisions in them. That is to say, if the first buyer receives notice that an acceptable offer is received from a third party, he has three to seven business days to make his offer noncontingent. Get tough here. Make it seventy-two hours, not three business days. Business days can sometimes run you into a whole week with holidays, weekends, and such.

Also, make sure notice to the agent is deemed as adequate. Don't allow yourself to be tied up with a contingent offer where you have to send out private detectives to find the first buyer to give him notice. Remember, you are granting a favor to the first buyer by even entertaining this kind of an offer. Don't allow him to put you in a defensive position where you have to track him down to give him notice.

Tip #5: *Always insist on nonrefundable earnest money (unless of course the financing falls through).*

In most cases the buyer will say no. But good contracts are structured that way. Try to get one. If you can't, ask that if for any reason, if the buyer cannot perform, the earnest money is nonrefundable. If he flatly refuses, ask why. What possible reason could there be outside of the ability to get a mortgage? Find out what reservations exist. If there is too much wiggling up front, you may have an insincere buyer who will cost you time and aggravation. You might be better off taking a pass.

Tip #6: *Don't get seller's remorse.*

After the deal is done get on with life and don't look back. Life is too short. This is not the time to play Monday morning quarterback. It is a stupid waste of time.

Just as there are many things that sellers should keep in mind to guarantee success, there are many things that buyers should keep in mind.

Strategies for Buyers

Tip #1: *Always work with a broker (unless you are an experienced buyer who's especially savvy in the particular market where you're looking).*

As we stated earlier, whereas the seller is primarily (and erroneously) concerned with bypassing a broker to save a commission, the buyer is going to pay for the service one way or another. Not only that, buying FSBO limits your selection, and you will be missing too many opportunities that might in fact be so much better than the one great house you might have stumbled across.

Tip #2: *Always use a mortgage broker.*

Dealing directly with a lender limits you to that one lender's products and guidelines. For no money at all, you can have someone else shop the mortgage market and get you the best rates and access to a wide range of products that might make more sense than one bank could offer. Why wouldn't you have someone else do the work for you, especially if it isn't going to cost you anything, and if it winds up saving you money because they got you a better deal than you could on your own.

Tip #3: *If your attorney isn't a real estate attorney, look elsewhere.*

I cannot underscore this one enough. Remember, if you needed a cardiologist you wouldn't hire a podiatrist.

Tip #4: *Use a home inspector.*

This is especially true if you are a first-time buyer who is new to the game. For the small fee inspectors charge, you will be getting peace of mind that the house you are buying isn't going to fall down around your ears the week after you close. Also, you will be getting a clear understanding as to what specific deferred maintenance you can expect down the line, say over the next five years. You will also be in a better position to know what to budget for those repairs and if you can afford them. By the way, make sure you go with the inspector when he does his inspection. It will be a valuable learning experience and you get to ask all sorts of questions that may seem really stupid. In some cases the inspector thinks they are, but you are more stupid if you don't ask them.

Tip #5: *Buy where you can afford now.*

Don't put it off until the market gets better. The market for buying is always right. That may not sound logical but it is if you consider the following:

1. There's no percentage in renting, ever. It is a short-term reality that is never a great idea financially.
2. Prices may be up today in your area, but if you wait you will be spending more money renting and will kiss the difference away in what you might have spent in rent versus buying and building equity.

Tip #6: *Don't hold out looking for the perfect deal.*

There is always a better deal around the corner, or at least one that your brother-in-law says is a better deal. Find a property that makes sense and buy it. Don't vacillate. Buy it. If you find a really good deal, you have done your research, and you have connected with a good broker in your area, that should be good enough. People waste so much time "what-if-ing" themselves to death. Here's another thing to remember: The absolutely best deals go to the brokers in most cases anyway, because they have the inside track. They see properties before they hit the market and the public has a chance to grab them. So if you really want to make yourself neurotic you might ask, "If this is such a great deal how come the broker didn't buy it?" The answer to that is simple: They can't buy everything in the store, can they?

Tip #7: *If you want a single-family home, buy a single-family home.*

If you want a two-family home, buy a two-family home. If you want a three-family home, buy a three-family home. I think you get the progression by now. The point is, buy what you want. Don't try to convert something that doesn't work into what you want. The cost to do so almost never makes good economic sense.

Tip #8: *Try to do a fifteen-year mortgage as opposed to a thirty.*

The difference in payments is surprisingly small and the savings, over the additional fifteen years, is astronomical. This is especially true if you think you are going to be in the house a long time. You build equity so much faster with a fifteen-year mortgage than you do with a thirty-year mortgage.

Tip #9: *If you have little or no money to buy a house, don't let that dissuade you from getting into the market.*

Talk to your broker. Talk to your mortgage banker. There are many programs for first-time buyers that let you get in for as little as $500 down and sometimes even less than that. (VA programs let you buy for nothing down.)

Tip #10: *Remember, the first house you buy is most likely not the last house you buy.*

So-called starter houses let you get into the game and build equity so you can really get your dream house down the road. The point is that you have to start somewhere. If you are holding off because you want to buy the perfect house *now*, and you don't want to trade up later, consider this: The average homeowner moves every seven years. If you are an average buyer, you will be out of that starter home sooner than you think. Seven years is nothing once you become a grown-up. Ask anyone with young children. They can't believe where the years went.

No, renting is not how you start. Buying is how you start. Everything changes when you buy a house. In many cases, it is a bigger commitment than going to school or taking a new job. However, the ability to own your own home is part of what makes this country great. It can also put you on the road to financial independence.

Tip #11: *Don't get buyer's remorse.*

Grow up. About five to ten minutes after the ink has dried on your contract you will get this funny feeling in the pit of your stomach and think to yourself, "What the hell have I done? How do I get out of this?" By midnight you will need a martini, a fifty-gallon drum of Prozac, or a psychiatrist. Relax. It is normal to be second-guessing yourself. It happens to everyone. Just don't wimp out and give in to this normal feeling by wavering in your decision. Remember, it made sense at the time you made the decision to buy and if your instincts were right then, they are right now. You won't regret it two years later.

Here's one last tip. Whether you are the buyer or the seller, it will serve you well. *Don't get greedy.* Please, please, please resist the impulse to get greedy. If you are a buyer, don't try to steal the property, and if the seller is selling for reasons that are personally distressing, don't be a bastard at the negotiating table. It will come back to haunt you in spades. Try to negotiate as if you were on the opposite side of the table and ask yourself, how would I feel if someone came in and proposed this to me. The "What are you, an idiot?" approach just doesn't make it. Even if you win in the short run, keep in mind that this is the community you are going to be living in and somehow it will come back to bite you.

Chapter 7

Open House Secrets

"Will you walk into my parlor?" said the spider to the fly.
—Mary Howitt

The open house: What's it all about? In many parts of the country, sellers and/or their agents elect to have a house they are trying to sell open to the public during particular times, usually on weekends with specific hours posted either on the sign or in local advertising. The theory is that this provides an opportunity for prospective purchasers to view the premises in an easygoing, low-pressure way. They can just walk right in and kick the tires all they want. The welcome mat is out for literally everyone.

Smart agents will actually go to the trouble of canvassing the neighborhood and inviting the people in the immediate area to "come on down." At the bare minimum, they should send postcards as invitations. They do this for several reasons. First of all, the curious "nosey neighbors" are going to come anyway. By inviting them, it shows those neighbors that the agent is hardworking and not going to take them for granted as possible buyers. You would be surprised how many sales are actually made to one of the neighbors, or to one of their friends or relatives. Haven't you ever had someone over to your house say something like "I love your house, and I just love this street." These types of qualified leads are what agents are banking on, and if they get lucky with this approach, it is a quick sale for them. It also provides them with the opportunity to get what is known as a "double dip." That's where an agent sells his own listing without the assistance of a cooperating broker. They make twice the commission that way.

Another reason agents solicit interest from the neighbors is that they could end up being a source of other homes to add to their listing inventory. Surely you have gone down streets and seen more than one house for sale. Sometimes you'll see a single agent with multiple properties being offered. Many sellers don't know whom to call when they look for an agent, so they just ride around and look to see which agent has the most signs up in their area. That's why it makes sense for an agent to work the area.

I often ask my agents how they can justify their time if *no one* shows up at their open house. (They call that "getting skunked," by the way.) They can get a return on their time, IF they have worked the neighborhood. Here's an example: The open house is scheduled for Sunday from 1:00 to 3:00 P.M. Starting Tuesday, the agent goes door to door with a dialogue something like this:

"Hi, I'm Jim Smith from ABC Real Estate, and I'm having an open house at the Jones's at 224 Sycamore this Sunday. I was wondering if you or anyone else in your family would like to take a look or stop by for a cup of coffee?"

Homeowner: "Oh, yes, I saw your sign."

Agent: "Yes, it's a great house. Do you know anyone who might want to buy it? This is such a great neighborhood."

Homeowner: "No, I don't."

Agent: "I see. Gee, it is *such* a nice place. You don't know anyone?"

You would be surprised at the positive responses agents get if they aren't pushy, say all of this with a friendly smile, and are sincere in their approach. Many times they will get a lead on the second attack by simply being persistent and asking, "You don't know *anyone?*" Sometimes the neighbors will be incredibly impressed that the agent would knock himself out in this manner. They will say things like, "Wow, you sure do work hard, don't you." This provides the smart agent with a great opening like, "Oh, yes, I promised the Jones family that I was going to do everything to get their house sold, and I don't want to take anyone for granted." Many times the neighbors will actually ask for the agent's business card, thinking, "Heck, this guy is good. If I ever need an agent, I know who I am going to call."

Stage Your Home for Maximum Appeal

Okay, so you, the would-be buyer, decides to enter this house that seems so inviting. What should you see? Well, if the agent has done his job, he will have the listing properly "staged." Barb Schwarz, a Realtor and trainer in the profession, teaches one of the most interesting and effective series of seminars on what she calls "staging a listing." Simply put, she shows agents how to make the house appear more saleable. It goes way beyond commonsense things like cleaning the house until it sparkles. It's more than telling the homeowner to remove all the clutter and paint the walls. She goes through every facet of how to make the house look its absolute best. She shows how to trim the hedges and brighten up the outside of the house for maximum curb appeal.

Staging a listing involves more than just appearance. Barb likes to remind agents that, "If you can smell it, you can't sell it." The sense of smell is one of the strongest of all of the senses. Many of us can think of certain aromas that when we smell them, there is a sense of something so familiar that we are simply transported back to the time and place where we originally smelled it. A smelly house turns off buyers tremendously. If they have looked at several houses they will even refer to one as "the one that smelled so badly from that old basset hound." Incidentally, I knock 10 percent off the price if a smoker has owned the house. Sorry folks, but that's the way it is. It's just one more good reason to quit that habit.

If bad smells don't sell, does that mean pleasant smells do? Smart agents think so. Anything the agent can do to enhance how the home shows is part of the deal. Some tricks of the trade: making chocolate chip cookies or baking bread. Is there any fragrance more inviting than bread baking in the oven? The chocolate chip cookie gig is even better because not only does the house smell like your loving grandma's, but your prospective buyers get to eat the cookies. This further adds to a positive sense memory and might move the house up a notch in a buyer's mind.

Another trick I like is potpourri cooking on the stove. Better still is placing a drop of vanilla extract on several light bulbs strategically arranged throughout the house. As the bulb heats up, the fragrance of the vanilla is released and wafts appealingly toward the unsuspecting nostrils of those heretofore not-so-serious "lookers." If there is a fireplace, there should always be a fire going. Seeing a fire burning in a fireplace conjures up a primordial sense of home and hearth.

Inside an Open House: The Agent's Agenda

So let's get back to this thing called the open house—what is it *really* all about? It probably seems like an obvious question. But is it? Agents have open houses for a number of reasons that may not be readily apparent. They want to sell the house. That's pretty obvious. Another reason an agent might do it (and this is the wrong reason) is to simply get the seller off his back. By doing an open house some sellers feel that the agent is working for them. However, the prime reason a smart agent does an open house is to increase their list of potential prospects.

Wait a minute. If you are the seller, are you saying that you might take exception to an agent using your house to cultivate his or her own book of business? Are you saying that it bothers you that the agent might take one of those buyers that just walked into your house and try to sell him another house? Well, if that's the case, might I suggest something? Get over it. Because that's what agents are doing and you may as well know it up front. When an agent decides to hold an open house at your home, he is setting up shop to sell a house. If it happens to be *your* house, then terrific. But don't have hurt feelings if you hear the agent say, "Yes, this is a great house, but what's that you say? You were looking for a house not quite as expensive (big, small, old) as this one? Well, as it turns out I happen to know of one that just came on the market over on, etc., etc."

Speaking of expensive, one of the things that will probably happen at the open house is that the agent may try to qualify different people who express interest in the home. As such, the agent will probably be equipped with a calculator, a yellow pad and pencil, and various qualifying forms to determine the financial viability of anyone that asks. The agent should also have various facts and figures about the house to help answer the prospect's more serious questions. Good agents should never answer, "I am not sure, let me check that out and I'll get back to you." They should have done their homework before the open house.

Remember, we mentioned that the listing should be staged. Agents should be staged, too. "Staged" means they should look the part and be appropriately and professionally dressed. They should also know their lines. They should know what they are talking about and everything there is to know about the house they are representing. I just hate it when I walk into an open house and the agent is reading the newspaper and when I ask a question he simply says, "It should be on the feature sheet." One of the assignments I give newer agents that work for me is to go around and take notes on how other agents conduct themselves at open houses. I tell them to watch, look, observe, and learn. Try to emulate what approach you admire and notice what agents do that seems unprofessional or ineffective. Watching other agents is an incredibly effective learning tool.

Some agents, simply from a business standpoint, should never do an open house. They have the personalities of tree slugs. They do little more than take up space and could be replaced by one of those "information" boxes you see in front of some houses. Other agents will tell you that one of the keys to their success is their ability to build rapport at an open house. I once asked one of my better agents why he thought he was so good at open houses and he told me, "Because I am there to sell the house. If I don't think I have a shot at selling the house at the opening, I won't do it." That agent was good because he knew how to sell. This may shock you, but not all agents do.

Deciding to Hold an Open House

Whose idea is it to do the open house in most cases? The seller or the agent? Surprisingly, it is usually the agent. You would think that the seller would say, "Hey let's get as many people as we can to come in and look at the house. Maybe we should just open it up and invite the world to come and take a good look." That would be very logical except for a few things. Generally, when a seller asks an agent to sell his house, he trusts that the agent will know what works best. If it is an "Open," fine. Usually what the seller wants is a slew of advertising. Advertise it to death. That's what they think is going to sell the house.

Sellers must subconsciously recognize that doing an open house is relatively cheap. It usually costs little more than the agent's time. That's not what they want. They want the broker to spend lots of money so they feel they are getting their money's worth. Paradoxically, any good agent will tell you that advertising doesn't sell homes. To be more precise, it rarely sells homes. What sells a house is a good agent with a well-priced home. Floyd Wickman says it in the reverse by stating, "All the servicing (and advertising) in the world can't sell an overpriced house." You can do a million open houses, but they won't sell your property if the price isn't right.

Can you get too much of a good thing? By that, I mean, can you do too many open houses? You bet you can. This is where the Venus flytrap catches the seller. I tell my agents, if the seller insists that you do an open house (I don't recommend them) there are very strict rules that have to be agreed to by both parties. The seller cannot have more than *one* open house a month. This is a good thing for the seller. Some sellers insist they want it open every Sunday, and Saturdays too. This is a big mistake.

Statistically, the number of sales made at open houses is very insignificant. In fewer than 5 percent of the sales does the buyer actually buy because of the open house. Most sales occur because of a sign and an agent. But that's not the issue here. The danger of doing too many open houses is that you will overexpose the property. Human perception is strange and very fallible. If a house is held open, the agent will usually place extra signs directing would-be purchasers to the home. Potential buyers that pass by will see the open house signs. After several weeks of passing multiple signs, their perception of time is affected and it seems like this house has been on the market longer than it actually has.

Where Do Buyers Come From?

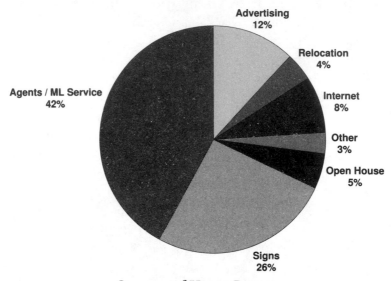

Sources of Home Buyers

Source: *National Association of Realtors: Home Buying and Selling Process, 2001.*

As you will note from the diagram, signs and agents clearly make for the greatest source of buyers. At 72 percent, the potential is almost three-quarters of all buyers. When you compare this with the meager return of an open house (5 percent), you are talking a difference of a factor of thirteen. Since the yield is statistically so low for an open house, it is obvious that the agent who does them at a seller's request must be banking on some other benefit for the investment of his or her time. One thing to also consider with respect to open houses is that even though the possibility of selling is low, 36 percent of all buyers out there use open houses as part of the process.

This doesn't mean that a potential buyer's perceptions aren't fallible. Here's another example of how they are manipulated. Let's say a driver approaches an area and sees several signs from the same broker (or better still, the same agent). The presumption is that this broker must be the broker to call in this area, because, heck, look at all the signs he has out there. Smart brokers make it a policy to try to get as many signs out there on highly traveled thoroughfares as possible. Drivers make the ultimate captive audience. Each time someone drives by the sign it makes an impression in the marketplace and (one hopes) on potential buyers. If an agent's advertisements make enough impressions they can seriously manipulate not only a market, but the public's perception of an agent's standing or credibility in that market.

I once heard a broker at a conference say that if you wanted to take over a market in the shortest time possible, you needed to have as a listing every piece of vacant land going in or out of the town in which you wanted to do business. He went on to say that you should list any property you could, regardless of how overpriced it was, simply to get real estate for your signs. Making those impressions in the marketplace was critical. In essence, what an agent should try to do is get lots of cheap billboard advertising all over town. If he had a myriad of signs out there with his name on them, anyone attempting to buy or sell in that particular market will think that this particular agent is the only game around. However, with more people using the Internet to buy and sell real estate, that reality is starting to shift. We'll look more later at the impact of the Internet on the buying/selling process.

Rules for a Successful Open House

Open houses do have their place, and they can be an effective part of your selling strategy. Lest you think that I'm completely dissuading you from using them, I've included the following guidelines that I have found to be critical to ensuring the success of an open house.

1. No more than one a month.
2. Potential buyers have to be able to find the house. If an

agent has to put up fifty different directional signs and hire native scouts so that people can find the place, then forget it.

3. The house has to be ready to be open to the public. Yes, I know, that sounds like common sense; unfortunately common sense is not that common. The house has to shine and glisten. It has to be in showroom condition. It has to be *market ready.*

4. The house has to have a reasonable chance of selling at the list price. This is not a fishing expedition. If the house is hopelessly overpriced, then don't hold the open house. If the seller wants to waste his time that's fine. The agent shouldn't.

5. The house has to be the kind of a house where the agent would like to have a chance of increasing the quality of his clientele.

With respect to number five here, remember we said earlier that one of the reasons an agent does an "Open" in the first place is to procure other business. If the agent sells the house, then great! If he doesn't, what does he have to show for his time? For example, let's say that the house is a bona fide dog, and on the wrong side of town. Frankly, some houses fit that description. If the agent is lucky, one of the prospects that comes through the house may just happen to want to buy it. If the agent is unlucky, he will wind up gathering more prospects that want to buy something similar. This keeps the agent selling down-market houses. If he or she wants to increase his revenue, he has to look for ways to increase the quality of his listing inventory.

Sorry folks, but I do think I mentioned somewhere earlier that this is a business. This may sound like it is entirely self-serving on the agent's part, but it isn't. What we have here is a quid pro quo. There is an exchange of something for something. The agent is giving up his time in exchange for giving the seller a shot at selling his house. Now you might balk and say, "Wait a minute, isn't that why the agent was hired in the first place?" I beg to differ. The agent was not hired to have open houses. The agent was hired to sell the house. Our handy-dandy pie chart clearly illustrates that having an open house is not the best way to sell houses. It is a marginally successful method at best. Hence, the realization of the quid pro quo.

Agents will do lots of things to help build rapport with prospects at open houses. Most of these are nothing more than strategies. Others are just effective sales techniques. (We'll discuss some of these in more detail in the next chapter.) So the next time you drive by one of those very inviting signs that say "Open House," try to be a little more aware that there is a far greater agenda going on than just having you stop by to say hello.

Chapter 8

The Negotiators:
The Talk of the Town

In the beginning, there was the word . . .

—John 1.1

eal estate deals are won or lost at the bargaining table. In our earlier discussion of FSBOs, we mentioned that the seller is at a clear disadvantage in this particular area of the arena. Indeed, the pro has a clear upper hand. Forgetting, for a moment, individual styles, which can vary like the spots on the leopard, let's start out with a basic premise. Who is the agent negotiating for?

I could get into book-length arguments on this point, but I won't. I could talk about buyer's agents, who negotiate for the buyers "only." I could talk about negotiating to best defend the seller's interest. All of that is interesting enough, but here's the real deal. Although it is true that the client's interest is kept first and foremost (and is held as sacrosanct), the agent who negotiates without keeping his own interest pretty high toward the top of the priority list makes for a pretty poor agent.

Sometimes you will hear honest agents tell you straight out, "Hey, I'm negotiating for me." To this comment many sellers would say, "I knew that. Agents are only interested in making a commission. They don't care what I get as long as they get paid." This is the core issue of what I am about to tell you in reference to negotiating.

Agents want to make a living. And you know what? They are entitled to make a living just as you are. They can't make a living, however, if the deals they negotiate continually undermine their client's position. It is only by putting those win/win scenarios together on a repeated basis that any agent worth his salt can build a good business.

Sometimes sellers feel that the negotiation has turned against them when they are getting less than they expected for their home. It hasn't. The negotiation is going along exactly as it should, as it rides with the current of the market. I will make a bold assumption and say the agent is probably not holding a gun to the seller's head. Is that a fair statement? At any point in a good faith negotiation, the seller can break off and say the magic word, *no*. The buyer can too. That's why it is called a negotiation. Now sometimes, sellers can raise very strong objections to the purchaser's style, or the agent's approach for that matter. This happens all the time, and it doesn't mean that somebody's interest has been subjugated or undermined. No matter how much of a stink the parties put up, a client's interest has been served as long as the fiduciary responsibility of confidentiality has not been breached. So the key to winning or cutting your best deal rests with being able to find the best agent and getting that invaluable individual on your side of the table. How you go about that will be discussed in the next chapter. For now let's discuss what it is that agents do, and just how they go about doing it.

Rapport Building in Negotiations

The key to all negotiations lies in the ability to establish rapport. Sometimes this falls somewhere on a resume, as the human resource mavens would like to call it, under "general people skills." It's a lot more than that. Effective negotiators put themselves in the other person's shoes. They have to either feel the other party's pain or give the illusion of knowing their pain (as well as their joy). The have to master the ability of becoming emotional and intellectual chameleons. They must have an almost intuitive understanding of how to foster rapport. This is no small feat.

If the negotiator, the facilitator of the deal, loses rapport with any of the players (even those idiots who should probably have their faces slapped), the deal runs a very high probability of dying. The agents who are the best in the field get paid the most, or should I say *earn* the most, because they are incredibly adept at mastering this skill. Principals almost by definition cannot do this because they are personally attached to the outcome.

What skills, either instinctive or learned, does the master negotiator use? To understand this we have to understand the subtleties of human communication.

Depending on what scientific treatises you read, you will find various percentages being used to designate the actual amount of communication that is done on a nonverbal level. As much as 80 to 90 percent of communication can be attributed to various nonverbal cues including facial expression, body language, and mannerisms. Some researchers say that the tone of the voice can account for as much as 38 percent of what is being communicated.

Smart communicators pick up on these nonverbal cues and use them to finely tune their best negotiating techniques. As such, being able to interpret and transmit nonverbal communication is essential for building rapport, which is the benchmark of effective negotiating.

Let me give you a few examples. One of the simplest techniques is called *matching*. In negotiating, the upper hand can change by consciously matching the other party's movements. Leaning forward, recrossing the legs, or speaking at the same speed or tonal quality as the opposing side can do this quite subtly. It is important to note that matching is not mimicking. Mimicking is not subtle at all. Your adversary will probably pick up on what you're doing, become wise to your movements, and might even move away. He could even take offense.

Every skilled agent learns in Negotiating 101 that the key to winning is getting agreement. If you can get your customer, your buyer, your seller, or whomever you happen to be working with at any given moment to start agreeing with you, you are well on your way to making whatever you want to happen take form. Agreement can take place on the most insignificant aspects of your agenda.

Sometimes deliberately putting up roadblocks on any agreements at all can work to your advantage. Remember the Paris peace talks of the early '70s to end the Vietnam War? The talks were hopelessly deadlocked before they had even really started. For months all the involved parties dragged their feet in an attempt to decide the shape of the table. They finally resolved that a circle would best serve their needs. Hanoi won the first victory because they knew that if they could keep the negotiations going long enough, time would be on their side and major concessions would easily fall their way. They recognized the situation of political unrest in the United States and knew that the Americans wanted a speedy end to the war. By stalling for weeks and months on end over the table issue, the North Vietnamese negotiators seized a clear advantage. The tactic is designed to establish a posture of superiority where one side is made to agree with the other over small details. Once a series of small details has been agreed to the larger issues become smaller still.

When we were talking about contracts back in Chapter 1, I mentioned the five P's and how most sellers presume that the only thing worth talking about is the price. We now know that many times this is actually not the case. If an agent for a buyer can get agreement on the four other determinants in a deal, the seller is much more inclined to move closer to the buyer's price than he might ever realize.

Many times a strong negotiator will even start nodding his head up and down ever so slightly to get the opposition to follow suit. This lures his adversary into matching the behavior. Soon every one is subtly nodding in agreement and saying, "Yes, Yes, uh huh, I see, no problem." Watch the next time you sit with an agent how she tries to get agreement even on what seems to be totally unrelated and insignificant facts and issues. It will start out with simple things like the weather. "Isn't this a great day?" "Boy that's a great view, isn't it?" This second statement is what Tom Hopkins, who is perhaps the greatest trainer of professional salespeople in America, calls a "tie-down." It is one of the strongest ways of getting closure with a client. After a series of tie-downs, a buyer literally closes himself and reaches for the pen. "That family room seemed big enough, didn't it?" "This payment is well within your monthly budget, isn't it?" "June won't be too late to close on this house, will it?" Note all the tie-downs. They start out small but they get you to the goal line. The negative tie-downs are especially effective. They have twice the subtlety because they make your pitch sound much more conversational, not like you are pressuring for agreement.

The tonal quality of the seller's voice is important too, as is his speed, or rate, of speech. If he is nervous and is speaking quickly in a high-pitched voice, the agent might match the speed and tone without being obvious. Gradually, as the agent attempts to sway the seller to his position, the speed might decrease and the pitch might drop a quarter octave. If the seller speeds up or raises the pitch, the agent follows, recognizing that he is losing rapport and quickly tries to reestablish his position of superiority. It is a fascinating process to observe. If you know the dance steps, it is especially fascinating. Watch for these little insights the next time you find yourself in a position where someone is trying to sell you something.

One of my favorite selling techniques is the "imbedded command." The imbedded command works like this. Rather than ordering someone to do this or that, you simply ask them to do it. "I wonder if I could ask you to look at this view." This is so much more powerful than saying, "Look at this view." Stronger still would be to pair the imbedded command with a tie-down. "I wonder if I could ask you to look at this view, would you?" Even if you hated the house, I cannot think of anyone who wouldn't take a look at the view after it was posed to them like that.

Ultimately the imbedded command leads up to, "I wonder if you would be good enough to sign here, would you?" Don't you think that this is more effective than simply saying, "Sign here"? I do. The imbedded command is most effective when the person is perceived as being an authority figure or a person in control of the situation. This is one of the reasons that I stress to my agents the importance of looking and dressing the part. If they look like professionals, these subtle cues work so much better. A properly attired agent in a dark navy blue suit projects power and authority; thus, when they politely ask you to do things you usually will comply. Maybe it is just using smooth sales techniques, but it is fun to know what is going on when it is happening to you.

Neuro-Linguistic Programming

Really smooth negotiators use another method of short-circuiting the response system. It is based on something called *Neuro-Linguistic Programming* (NLP).

One of the tools skillful practitioners use to hone their abilities is something called the Representational Bias Test. It is designed to help one determine what his primary or secondary mode of communication is. Armed with this knowledge, a really accomplished rapport builder can slip in and out of his opponent's mode, matching it as the conversation moves along. If it sounds complicated, it isn't. With a little practice and thought, anybody can do it. Let me explain how this works.

Have you ever wondered why you just get along with some people more easily than others? It is probably because they have the same primary modes of communication as you do. They might be visual people. They might be people who primarily are auditory. That might be people who are "touchy-feely," or what we call kinesthetic. Or they might be your classic "accountant or engineer" types, the digital folks. The words that a person uses betray their preference.

A person who says to you, "I don't know, something just doesn't *sound* right here," would clearly be auditory. A person, who instead stated, "Something just doesn't *look* right to me," would conversely be a visual person. How about the same thought expressed this way: "Hey, this just doesn't add up." That's right. That's the digital personality. Likewise, the kinesthetic person might express his thoughts this way: "I don't know, but something just doesn't *feel* right here."

Really skilled negotiators recognize when rapport is broken or becomes incongruent. They pick up on the verbal cues when one person begins speaking in one mode while the other individual is in another. It is an incredibly valuable skill. Try it with your significant other sometime, especially when the discussion starts to heat up.

I once saw a woman who was all set to buy a car. She really was. I could just tell. She went to get behind the wheel so she could get a sense for just how the car would feel. She had been talking about the leather, how rich and expensive it felt. Suddenly, the salesman (I suppose in an effort not to appear sexist) asked her if she knew how many cubic inches of horsepower were under the hood? Was she aware of how many pounds of torque would be directed to the positraction rear wheels when she shifted from second to third at 5,000 RPMs? Did she care? When Mr. Digital meets Mrs. Kinesthetic we have here what we might call a "failure to communicate." Needless to say, not only did the woman not buy the car, she couldn't wait to get out of the showroom.

I remember seeing an episode of *Star Trek: The Next Generation* where one of the characters was half-Betazoid. Betazoids could supposedly feel what others were feeling around them. Hence, they could tell when a person was nervous or being untruthful. This particular character was a negotiator who was trying to resolve a longstanding conflict between two bellicose planets. Another Betazoid objected when she became aware that this person's power was being used without the knowledge of the members of the other faction. In the same way, it could be argued that persons trained in the neuro-linguistic approach are taking advantage. You can draw your own conclusions, though as Floyd Wickman, real estate trainer "par excellence," once said, "The difference between a con and a salesman is intent." But next time you are in a conversation, listen for the cue words and try to determine what mode the other person is currently in. Once you have that established, try shifting into that mode and see how the line of communication flows.

Earlier in my own sales career, I would wrestle with different kinds of prospects. Some prospects I just seemed to connect with easily, while I couldn't connect with others no matter what I tried to say. I now realize that my style was simply incongruent with theirs. As it turns out, I am primarily an audio person with a strong secondary orientation in the visual mode. Things just have to sound right for me to be persuaded. I was up against impossible odds whenever I would try to interact with accountant types. Now I automatically switch gears. I start talking about square footage, floor ratios, assessed valuation, return on investment, income before overhead, cost savings on R-30 insulation . . . details, details, details. Who cares that I am an audio person?

Certainly not these hardcore digital types. Trust me, we get right on the same page when I start addressing them in the language they want to hear (or can *understand* best) rather than the one I am comfortable speaking. Does it take effort? You bet, but not all that much, really. But the results have astounded even me at times.

Listen to the next conversation with anyone that comes along. Note the frequency of the words that seem to be in the same mode. If you're still not sure how it works, look at the list of these twelve words below and try to identify the mode.

1. Exact
2. Differential
3. Inordinate
4. Aroma
5. Smooth
6. Brittle
7. Loud
8. Cacophony
9. Acerbic
10. Bright
11. Sunny
12. Gorgeous

If you're still confused, the first three are digital; 4 to 6 are kinesthetic; 7 to 9 are auditory; and the last three are clearly visual.

If you would like to take the actual complete test, you will find it in a book called, appropriately enough, *Magic of NLP Demystified*, by Byron Lewis and R. Frank Pucelick. The Representational System Bias Test is excerpted from *Magic Demystified* by Byron Lewis and Frank Pucelik (Metamorphous Press, 1991).

How Negotiators Try to Close the Deal

Not only have modern-day negotiators honed these skills for reading people to razor sharpness, but the really good ones are masters of closing techniques as well. Twenty-five years ago, I learned from a master salesman and negotiator to "close often, and early." There is no downside to closing. Closing is a good thing because it clarifies what the buyer wants. It also rules out what he or she doesn't want. In fact, if the negotiator doesn't determine what is not of interest, he cannot move on to what is of interest.

I absolutely love to see a salesperson try to sell *me*. Sometimes I come off as slightly obnoxious because I will say, "I can't believe it! You're doing an order blank close on me." This, by the way, is one of the simplest and most effective closes in use. It works as follows. The agent or salesperson simply asks questions about what you want or don't want, and starts filling in the order blank. In a real estate transaction this would be the Contract of Sale or the binder statement. Ask enough questions and the prospect closes himself, and all the agent has to do is hand him a pen and say, "Sign here."

Sometimes the prospect gets a little wiggly and says, "Wait a minute, I didn't say I was going to buy anything . . . I'm not ready to buy." With an order blank close, the agent just keeps going and says things like, "Oh, I know, I was trying to get your thoughts clearly on paper. It just helps me resolve in my own mind exactly what you wanted. I realize you don't want to buy just now. By the way, when did you say you wanted to move? Good, let me just make a note of that." (That last note becomes the closing date of the contract.)

Here are eleven of my other favorite closes. Including the order blank close, we'll call that Close #1, this gives you an even dozen.

Close #2: The Lost Cause Close

This one is really schmaltzy and therefore one of the most powerful. Here the salesperson appears to simply give up, he concedes that he is beaten. "You've won." It goes something like this: "You know, Mrs. Williams, I work hard at this business, perhaps too hard. I've tried everything to help find you the house of your dreams, and I guess I just don't know how to help you any more. We've looked at this kind of house and that kind of house. We have considered every possible style of home and every neighborhood within your price range. Where have I gone wrong? It's important for me to know. Could you explain what I could have done better so I won't make the same mistake twice?

After they hear this, most prospects can't wait to tell the agent everything they have done wrong (in the most compassionate way, of course). They will close themselves.

Close #3: The Ask a Question, Get a Question Close

Whenever a prospect asks a question, the agent follows it up immediately with another question. This reinforces commitment. Here's how it works. Let's say a customer asks, "Can I find a two-story, three-bedroom house in this price range? I'd like to keep my kids in the same school district." The agent asks, "Is this the only neighborhood you are willing to consider?" Let's presume they say yes. The next three-bedroom house the agent shows them (in that neighborhood) entitles him to go for the close. After all, they said that this was the neighborhood they wanted.

Close #4: The Summary Close

The major close is merely a collection of smaller ones. "Let me summarize what we have talked about. You like the home on Bailey, but which do you prefer . . . the one on Maple or the one on Bailey?"

Close #5: The Alternative Close

This close offers the buyer a choice, which may result in a subsequent offer or closing on a home. Here are a few examples. Move-in date: "Would you prefer moving in right away OR would ninety days from now be better?" Cash versus a mortgage: "Would you like to make this purchase with 20 percent down conventional financing or will you be paying cash?"

Close #6: The Erroneous Conclusion Close

This is one I like. It works best when a deep rapport has been established. In an effort to help the prospect better define his or her needs, the agent purposely makes an erroneous statement about something that has already been confirmed with him. Let's presume the prospect has narrowed the choice down to one property, the house on Elmwood. The agent might say, "Let's see now, how much do you think you would like to offer on that house on Sycamore?" The prospect quickly corrects the agent. The agent responds, "Oh yes, I'm sorry, the house on Elmwood, my mistake, let me make a note of that (on the order blank)." You can see how easily the agent can gain or strengthen commitment this way.

Close #7: The Wise Old Ben Franklin Close

This is so old, but it is just as powerful today as when Ben first did it. It works even better if the agent comes totally clean and says, "You know, we probably shouldn't do this, this is one of the oldest selling tricks in the book, it's called the Ben Franklin close." If the prospect hasn't heard of it, it makes the opening line an even more powerful rapport-building device because now the agent has let him in on one of her secrets. Here's how it works. Whenever he had to make a really difficult decision, Old Ben would draw a line down the middle of the page, and he would list all the Pros on one side and all the Cons on the other."

By actually drawing the line and explaining the process of how Old Ben would do it (in a sort of crackle-barrel manner), the prospect will usually close himself and list more reasons why he should buy (or sell). If the Con side of the page vastly outweighs the Pro side, then at least at that point, the agent can move on to where her energies will be better directed (e.g., a different property, revised terms, whatever is the scope of the negotiation at that time).

Close #8: The Secondary Question Close

The agent asks a question regarding a major decision, and immediately follows with a minor point question. A simple case would be where the agent asks, "So I guess we have a major decision here, should we go ahead on Smith Street? Or is Jones the right house for you? By the way, will you be going for a thirty-year mortgage or will you try to do a fifteen?" After responding to the minor point, the prospect is subconsciously acquiescing to the major point.

Close #9: The Similar Situation Close

This is a close that is brought out when the agent seems to be going nowhere. He can't seem to get any kind of commitment no matter what he does. Beware of these three words: *feel*, *felt*, and *found*. "Folks, I know making decisions like this can be pretty scary. I know this sounds like a lot of money, but I worked with a couple of people that were very much like you, not too long ago. They were scared, they didn't think they could afford the payments, they were just like you in a number of ways. I'm sure when they were looking at houses, they probably could *feel* that big bite in their stomachs and *felt* exactly like you do right now. But you know what they have *found?* Now that they are living in the house, all that pain and uncertainty is gone. What you're feeling right now is perfectly normal." The *feel, felt, found* close, as I like to call it, has saved me so many times, I cannot begin to tell you. It's corny but incredibly persuasive.

Close #10: The Take Away Close

Very old, very effective, very powerful. When the agent wants to turn up the heat a little, she uses the take away. "Yes, that would be a good house for you, but we had better not even consider this one, there has been much too much interest on this one and you are probably not able to move quickly enough to get an offer in; let's look at something else. It's just so awful to get your hopes up on something only to be disappointed. Really, we should look at that one over on Pierrepont Street instead." If the agent really wants to work you over, she'll put a tie-down at the end by saying, "Don't you think?"

Close #11: The Isolation Close

This is used when the prospect thinks he can get away. "No, we're not sure, we'd like to think about it overnight." The prospect usually breathes a sigh of relief, as this statement has easily blown the wind out of most salespeople. The skilled negotiator then moves closer and says, "No problem, I can appreciate that, Mr. Fishman. After all, this is a pretty big decision. You should think it over very carefully—boy, I know I would. So may I assume you will give this investment very careful consideration? Just to clarify my thinking, what phase of this opportunity is it that you want to think over? Is it the price? Are the terms too difficult? Is there a problem with the down payment?" It takes chutzpah for the agent to pursue the prospect to this degree. That's why it is called sales and that's why not everyone can make a six-figure income doing it. Most agents fold at the first, "I'd like to think it over."

Close #12: The Simple Trial Close

Remember, I was taught in my early days to close often and early. That's what is meant by the trial close. Agents and negotiators should always be looking to get agreement and commitment on anything and everything. "So did you like that house better than the last one? What did you like about that last one?" (Who said they liked that last one anyway?) By gathering a series of small closes it eventually leads to the big close—the signature on the contract.

By the way, in all these closes, really effective real estate negotiators rarely use words like contract. It's an agreement. Lawyers use contracts. People like you and I make agreements. I guess that's why we're so agreeable. You might also notice a certain reluctance to say things like, "Sign here!" That's not what we call user-friendly. The skilled negotiator likes to work with a soothing touch and get you to do the same thing by politely asking you to sign. They do this by saying, "I wonder if you would be kind enough to just authorize the paperwork down at the bottom? Would you do that for me, yes that's right, there and there, and don't forget to put your initials on the second page, please." (Note the imbedded command.) Another way of saying it is, "Now, I wonder if you would do us both the favor of putting your *John Hancock* right there."

If you want to have fun with the smoothest of negotiators, there is one surefire short circuit maneuver. When you recognize that you are being closed all over the place, simply respond, "I don't know." Tilt . . . Tilt . . . Tilt! "Well, what do you mean, you don't know? What don't you know?" Look at him blankly and shake your head and say, "I just don't know." Do this several times until it gets old. The agent will presume he's working with an idiot and will probably just leave you alone. There is absolutely no defense against the "I Don't Know Maneuver," as long as the prospect maintains his position and doesn't fold. I must admit, I have done this on occasion just to see salespeople sweat.

Now you have an overview of how skilled negotiators get you to do some of the things you didn't know you wanted to do. Watch for them. Try not to smile or giggle when you catch them in the act.

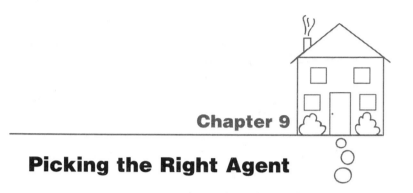

Chapter 9

Picking the Right Agent

Days off. —Spencer Tracy, when asked about what he looks for in a script

irst of all, rarely do buyers actually go out and look for an agent. They usually just stumble over them. At a cocktail party they may mention to someone that they are thinking of buying a house, and—wham!—someone at the party just happens to be in the business. Perhaps they mention it to a friend or relative and that person turns them on to someone in the business. In any event, it is a haphazard approach at best.

If the buyer is at the stage where he is actually looking at houses or calling on ads, other possibilities arise. Let's say a buyer walks into an open house. There is a nice friendly person sitting right there who is willing to sell them that house; there is even the possibility that the agent might be the right one for the buyer. This could be true for this house or another property. In any event, all of these approaches require the greatest elements of luck. Try to see if you can do a little better and maximize your chances for finding the best agent you can.

If you're looking at open houses and you come across an agent who seems nice, that's fine. How do you know if he is any good? What should you look for, what do you need? Whose interest will he represent? To explore these questions, let's consider the agent population in general. Here's the scoop: The average real estate agent in the field today represents probably the highest degree of mediocrity you will find in any business. The big issue that leads me to conclude that this may be a business fraught with mediocrity is the average annual income, which in many cases is based on an individual working "full-time," not "part-time." Based on the National Association of Realtors own statistics, the typical agent makes less than $10,000 a year. This now leads me to the first decision you will need to make about the agent you want to work with (presuming you want to make a choice).

Brokers and managers have wrestled with this dilemma as well. Ideally, most of them would prefer to be surrounded by the most professional team of agents they could find. All of them would be full-time, well-trained top producers. Given the choice, owners and managers would mostly prefer to have full-time people on their staffs. Why is that? It's really quite simple. I use this analogy: "You wouldn't want a part-time brain surgeon, would you?" No, if you needed that serious an operation, you would want the best doctor and the best medical team you could find, wouldn't you? It is the same thing in any selection you might make for professional help. All of these choices, whether it concerns your health or buying a home, deal with potentially life-altering ramifications. That's why you want somebody who is serious about his or her business. You want somebody who does it for real.

Many times, brokers will compromise their own good sense and take on a talented part-time agent by saying that they accept people who want to make a full-time "commitment" to the business: It is not the number of hours that makes for the quality of the business. I myself have said this and believed it, or at least used it to rationalize making that decision. I was never really comfortable with that choice. I can recall having a very competent agent that used to work for me. She was a full-time elementary school teacher (and an exceptional one at that). In addition, she was a phenomenal agent who consistently sold between two to three million dollars worth of real estate, year in and year out. What made her even better was that she always got very high marks from her customers and clients as well. She was an exception. But ideally, you want a full-time agent. There are very few exceptions out there.

To find the best agent, what you need to examine closest is not his profile but his R-E-C-O-R-D. Here's a handy acronym.

Recommendation

When you look for representation, or an agent to work with, you shouldn't just trust that the perfect person will drop into your lap. You are hiring someone. You wouldn't hire the first guy who asked for the job in other situations, would you? You need to interview them. Ask your friends and neighbors. Do they know a good Realtor? Do they know any that they would specifically recommend? Do they know any that you should avoid? Believe me, if they have had any bad experiences, they will be sure to tell you about them. If you needed a doctor and didn't know any, wouldn't you ask around? Sure you would. If you really got stuck, wouldn't you ask the Chamber of Commerce, the Better Business Bureau, the motel manager, and the person at the convenience store? I'll bet you would ask somebody. It might even be someone in your church. The list of people who might know someone who is good at what they do, be it a doctor or a Realtor, is probably endless. Ask and consider all recommendations. That should help you arrive at a better decision. It will at least increase your odds of getting a better agent more than the random approach. Unfortunately, it is still no guarantee.

Here's a better way. Ask people if they know of any good real estate companies in the area. You're not looking for an agent yet. Once you have resolved in your own mind that the information on the best companies has been supplied to you, call one high on the list. Ask to speak to the manager or the broker owner. When you get that person on the phone, tell him or her what your situation is (first-time buyer, new to the area, trade-up buyer, house to sell, etc.). Ask him, based on your particular set of circumstances, whom they would recommend if they were in your shoes. That's your best shot at getting the best match for your needs, agent wise.

Expertise

If you are stumbling across agents or having friends recommend their friends, you need to pay attention to this key issue. Not all agents are experts in the area you need. They may be great, but they may be working a different geographical market entirely. They may be the best residential specialists in town, but you might need a good commercial broker. They can be the best high-end broker you can find, but he/she might be lousy at working with first-time buyers.

With real estate agents, just like with doctors, there are specialties within specialties. Just as one doctor will recommend another doctor, a really good agent will not hesitate to recommend another agent if he thinks that that agent's expertise is better suited to the task. These agents will be smart enough to put themselves in for a little referral fee, but don't kid yourself on that point. I tell agents all the time, especially with respect to geography, "to refer it out." Unless the agent can maximize his own return on the investment of their time, I tell him to refer it out and leave the long distance driving to someone else. As a rule of thumb, the advice I give my agents with respect to this issue is, "If you don't know where it is, and you can't easily find it on the map, you should probably look for an agent who knows that market better than you do. And look for a 25 percent referral fee, while you're at it."

Expertise also has to do with tenure in the business. Is the agent brand-spanking new, or is he older than time? Neither should be your first choice. Let's think about our brain surgery comparison again. If you needed to have someone cut into your scalp, who would you want, the person who was number one in his class at Harvard Medical school, or the doctor who came highly recommended to you and had performed the operation hundreds of times before?

You want an agent who has done it before, and many times over. That way when something complicated or scary comes up, he will know how to deal with it. It is bad enough that *you* will be losing it. You don't need your agent having a panic attack, too.

Commitment

We touched on this. How committed to getting the task done is the agent you are interviewing? As for full-time versus part-time, you know my feelings on this by now.

Office

I told you to find the best real estate company around. Another way to ask this is, "Where is the best real estate office?" Now I am not talking about the physical office. That's important too, it just isn't the crucial issue. An OFFICE usually connotes, to people in the business, a group of agents. Just as a church is not just a building, an office is not just a space. A really good office has a synergy, an almost perceptible hum to it. People in town know about it. Agents in an office know about it and frequently leave one firm to go to another just so they can be associated with a group of winners as opposed to, ahem, the other guys.

Visit the office if you can. Feel the vibes and see how the operation works. It is one of the best ways to increase your chances of finding the best agent. I told you before to ask the manager (broker owner). Here's something that's even better. Call the manager and tell her your situation and tell her you would like to meet her "pick" the next morning at 9:00 at his office. You will be respected for being a person who means business and the manager will give you not just the royal treatment but the best agent bar none.

Reputation

Reputations, good or bad, are earned. They are earned by doing good work and having the proper credentials. Many agents sport fancy designations like GRI or CRS after their names. The first one means that they are a Graduate of the Real Estate Institute. This means they have taken an extra five courses of study in real estate that are above and beyond the statutory requirement. The GRI courses are excellent, and agents are given special credit they can use to fulfill any continuing educational requirements they may have. Oddly enough, most states have terribly low educational requirements to become a licensed real estate agent. New York's is relatively difficult and still only insists on a minimum of forty-five hours of pre-licensing training. A masseuse, by contrast, needs 650 hours, and a nail technician needs 450 hours.

Agents with the GRI designation are well regarded in the business. It is no guarantee of performance though. I have seen agents with GRIs who truly could not sell bread in a famine. Objectively speaking, the GRI courses are valuable and offer very good training for those who want to improve themselves in the business.

Another designation is the CRS (Certified Residential Specialist). This is the next degree up from the GRI, and indeed the GRI is a prerequisite for the CRS. Here we have another series of very intensive courses designed to give an added dimension to a real estate professional's practice. The point again, though, is that the designation is not a clear guarantee of performance. There are lots of doctors out there with post-doctoral medical degrees whom I would not feel safe with at all. If you see any other designations, ask the agent or the manager what he means. The list is endless.

I saw one agent who had so many letters after his name I presumed he had to be totally incompetent. Guess what? He was. The sad part about our business is, like other fields, we have what I call education junkies. The best way to discern an agent's reputation is to review any letters of recommendation or commendations the manager may have with respect to a particular agent.

Drive

Also known as determination. Many agents will have all sorts of awards and plaques hanging on their walls. That's usually a good sign. At least it means they are top performers. Be careful of a few things, however. Ask about the agent's performance not just based on volume but on style. Many agents sell millions upon millions of dollars worth of real estate each year, but you might not want to work with them. Sometimes managers refer to them as 800-pound gorillas. They may be top producers who care nothing about the quality of their "book." They might sell five million and have three million in folds. Managers know that agents like these are the kind that like to throw stuff against the wall to see how much will stick. You don't want to work with these people. You want your agent to have drive but not a blood lust. Consult with the manager and express your concerns with respect to the drive issue. This becomes important if there is an additional issue of part-time versus full-time. He can have all the drive in the world, but he is not around because he has to work the second shift at McDonalds, you could have a problem.

More Tips for Picking an Agent

Here are some other tips beyond those in R-E-C-O-R-D. If you are looking to sell your house, be aware of a little statistic the manager can give you called the *list/sale ratio*. I also call it the agent's kill ratio. This is, the specific ratio of success for all the listings an agent takes, and how many of them actually sell. If the agent has a ratio over 70 percent and all else seems right, hire him. You might probe further to find out what that agent's average time on the market is versus the rest of the market. Remember this: You are the boss. You need to tell the agent what you expect. He conversely needs to advise you of what he expects from you.

If I were selling a house (me personally), I wouldn't want the agent giving me constant feedback as to what potential buyers were saying about my house. Just call me when they want to put in an offer. Many sellers want to be told how each prospect hated the wallpaper and the decor and this and that. Please spare me the pain. Just tell me the price. Show me the money. Either way, you are the boss and you need to tell the agent how you would like him to work with or for you. If you want every detail, blow-by-blow, and every ounce of feedback, that's fine. Go ahead. Be a masochist.

Here's another pitfall to watch out for when looking for an agent. Many times a prospective buyer will call an office and inquire about a house. The person who answers the phone in many cases is an agent who is on phone duty, or what is sometimes called "opportunity time." It is kind of like the "UP" system in an automobile showroom or a department store. You call in on their turn. Finding a good agent this way would be relying on a high degree of luck.

In fact, there are many who would argue that the odds that the right agent for you will answer the phone are especially small; chances are against you because the best agents frequently do not take "floor time." They are too busy working their own accounts and client base. However, I have managed to get a good agent off the phone, but that type of luck isn't typical, and truthfully, I have seen agents on the phone who would embarrass any broker and who I would not wish on my worst enemy. Okay, I take that back. They might not have been *that* bad. Perhaps I'll just say that they would not have been my first pick if I were looking for an agent for myself or someone else who was important to me.

All that being said, here is how I would recommend selecting a real estate agent who is a good all-around general practitioner. First of all, I would choose an agent who was not new, with a minimum of five years in the business. You want someone who is hungry. He or she probably averaged between 2 and 5 million in closed sales in the previous year. You don't want anyone who is dabbling in real estate as a second income or part-time. (Remember what the C in R-E-C-O-R-D stands for: *commitment*.) Agents who closed less than that are not hungry enough; more than that and they start to become too concerned with their interest and not yours.

But what is the biggest single factor for making a selection? You've probably already guessed it. You want someone with a good bedside manner. You want that in a doctor, and you should want it in a real estate agent. If the agent in question only sold one and half million but is good during your one-on-one interactions, he or she can still be "in like Flynn." One last thing: If the agent has a vanity license plate, take a pass, and get someone else. He is too full of himself and will spend more time telling you about how impressive he is, and not enough time addressing the task at hand.

An issue even more important than the agent himself is the company he works for. What is the company going to do for you? If you are selling, you want the agent to supply you with a true marketing plan in writing. You want specifics with respect to what he will do, what he won't do, and when he will do it. You may not even agree with what he is proposing to do for you. Nevertheless, it is just as important to get those concerns on the table, too. If you go to the doctor, hopefully you discuss your condition and the kinds of treatment that are being recommended. There are various treatments and procedures for most conditions. These can include change in diet, exercise, drugs, surgery, and more. It could be some combination of all of these. In the same way that you should become involved with the prescribed and recommended treatment for your health, you also should have some input into how the marketing of your house should unfold.

However, let me be clear about what I mean by having input. Let the agent do his job the same way you would let the doctor do her job. It's all right to ask questions and show some involvement. But if you have hired him to do a job, and you trust that he can do that job, let him. And one final word, never, and I mean *never*, pick an agent (if you are a seller) based on the highest selling price quoted or the lowest commission. If someone tells you your house should sell for X, make sure that agent makes a very persuasive argument to prove to you that this is the correct price for the home. Swallow your pride, listen, and try to be truly objective as if you were a jury member. As far as commissions go, if you want cheap you can always get cheap. I always tell prospective sellers my fee is 7 percent of the sale price. When they say they can get it for 6 percent, I tell them if they can't find someone to do it for 5 percent or even 4 percent, they haven't called enough people. I tell them that my fee is what it is, and then I tell them why I charge what I do.

There will always be agents out there willing to list your house for a commission that is less than what you think it should be. There are always agents who are willing to undercut another agent. In most cases these agents can list the property quite well. Selling it is an entirely different matter altogether. And the truth is that their costs are about the same as mine. If they price themselves too cheaply, they cannot offer the same kinds of services that either I or a better competitor can offer.

What about buyer's representation? Do you need it? You might be well advised to consider this kind of an agent if you are new to an area and need to be seriously concerned with resale. Otherwise, I think the need for an advocate on the buyer's side of the transaction is greatly exaggerated to the point of bordering on the ludicrous. If you do go this route, make sure you get an advocate who is gentle and persuasive. Surly and obnoxious does not an advocate make. Remember, you are entering into an adversarial relationship with the seller. The last thing you need is someone who will be so bull-headed that he will negotiate you out of the deal before the deal ever gets struck.

In conclusion, when looking for an agent, ask around, interview several candidates, and know what to look for. Most importantly, trust your instincts and never forget that you're the boss.

Chapter 10

The Home Inspection

I want a house that has got over all its troubles; I don't want to spend the rest of my life bringing up a young and inexperienced house.

—Jerome K. Jerome

t is amazing how insecure the public has become over the last twenty years. Years ago people bought lots of products and most of them worked reasonably well and people slept pretty soundly. A generation or so ago we entered the age of the consumer and people became more litigious. Ralph Nader has been virtually deified, and the world has entered a perpetual state of paranoia. It's sad to say, but today everyone is convinced that anyone who is selling something is a crook or a liar or, at the very least, out to bamboozle their customers. This is true whether the item is a waffle iron, a fancy car, or a well-appointed house in the suburbs. Because of this perception an entire field within the real estate industry has emerged. Welcome to the home inspection business.

Have you ever seen those ads that usually appear in the back of magazines like *Popular Mechanics* or the *National*

Enquirer? "Become a Home Inspector, make up to $100,000 a year, part-time or full-time, etc." You might even see them in the Business Opportunities section of the classifieds. What's going on here? Don't you have to be an engineer or pass some serious licensing tests? Don't you have to have years of rigorous training in electrical contracting and foundation work? The answer might surprise you, because the correct answers to these questions are no, no, no, and no. (I think I got the right number of no's). Here's the deal: Anybody with a business card can say he or she is a home inspector. This industry within an industry is totally unregulated in just about every municipality I know of. You don't need a license, and since you are only required to give an opinion as to the condition of a house (a highly subjective opinion, I might add), who is to say your opinion is wrong?

Now don't let me mislead you here. There are many wonderful home inspectors who are more than qualified to render an opinion. However, because there are so few regulations and requirements in this profession you really need to be careful in picking an inspector. Often you might be looking for a structural engineer. Very few home inspectors are structural engineers, and the requirements to become one are much more stringent. I am often amused when builders come into my office during a lull or their slow season and tell me, "Oh, by the way, I do home inspections too."

The implication is that if they can build houses, they should be able to spot flaws in another person's work or in the typical resale house. Maybe they can, and maybe they can't, but the answer to this one is the classic, "Who knows?" So how do you pick a good home inspector, and how do you make sure you just didn't get somebody that bought a home inspection franchise two weeks ago?

As an aside, the going rate for a home inspection franchise is currently anywhere from $5,000 to $15,000. It comes complete with extensive training that can run from a week to two months.

Whom should you ask when you're looking for a referral for a home inspector? Oddly enough, I suggest that you should ask your real estate agent. The esteemed news show *60 Minutes* differed with me on this point when they gave a scathin͛ indictment of the home inspection business that was, in my opinion, really quite misleading. They reported a case where everyone was truly in cahoots, from the agent to the home inspector to the appraiser. It was a terrible example of finding the most egregious case of skullduggery you could find. Let's consider this more closely, shall we?

Above all else, the agent wants to make a sale and close the deal as smoothly as possible. Agents, in almost all cases, are not going to seek out a home inspector who will outright lie about the condition of a property. It simply isn't worth the risk of losing a license or being subject to criminal prosecution. The smartest thing you can do is to ask the agent for a list of home inspectors and discuss the pros and cons of each. Please note the agent is not supposed to recommend one over another. (Psst! Agents do recommend particular home inspectors all the time. However, in my humble opinion, this offense falls into the category of venial sins.)

What to Look for in a Home Inspector

Here's what I look for in a home inspector. By the way, I recommend that every person buying a house should hire one. Why? So they can make an intelligent decision to buy or not to buy based on the condition the inspector's report gives them. An inspection is not meant to be a deal-killer or a weapon for renegotiating, which seems to be what has happened throughout the real estate business.

The inspector who will do the best job is someone who has inspected a lot of houses (200 or more is a good starting point). A good inspector also might be a member of the National Association of Home Inspectors (a self-governing

body of better home inspectors that is responsible for policing its own). There is an American Society of Home
Inspectors (ASHI), too.

Home inspectors should give you a written report, and
they should insist that you are present during the actual
inspection. Notice I said *you*. This doesn't mean your kids,
your mother-in-law, or your nephew who is a college
freshman and is thinking of becoming an architect someday. It means *you*, the person who is buying the house, no
one else. If not, we really are talking about the case of too
many cooks spoiling the soup.

Something else you should look for in an inspector is
a good bedside manner. The home inspector should not be
an alarmist. Ask the agent. "Is this guy going to make me
more neurotic than I already am?" The inspector should be
able to explain things in a relatively calm and direct manner. He or she should be able to communicate in *layman's*
terms what is wrong with the property. Bear in mind, no
property is perfect. If you are looking for an inspector to
come up with a punch list of everything that is wrong with
the property, that's quite a different thing from your typical
inspection. Agents know which inspectors are wackos and
which ones do their jobs in a competent and professional
manner. Ask them. They are more on your side than you
will ever know.

Another reason I suggest that purchasers have an
inspector go through the house is because if they want to
buy it and live in it, maybe for the rest of their lives, they'll
sleep better knowing what to expect five years down the
road. If they purchase the house subject to an inspection
and subsequently elect not to purchase the house (in three
to five business days) that's okay too. They've eliminated
one more choice, and they can narrow the field that much
more. They're also more savvy about what to look for in
the next house.

Some Serious Don'ts

What should you *not* do when making a decision about an independent home inspector?

1. *Don't* pick an inspector who is also willing to do the repairs himself or who suggests others for the job. This is a clear conflict of interest and can lead to someone feathering his own nest.

2. *Don't* pick a home inspector based on price. If you buy cheap, you get cheap. If you get something for nothing, it is probably worth about the same.

3. *Don't* pick an inspector who doesn't maintain errors and omissions insurance. If an inspector screws up, and the house does in fact need an entirely new basement you hadn't budgeted for, it's nice to know that somebody might be covered.

4. *Don't* panic when you see the report. Discuss the findings or concerns that the report cites. These reports by their very nature make every house sound like they are falling into the ground. Any inspector who is worth his fee should be more than willing to explain whatever might have popped up.

5. *Don't* be afraid to comparison shop for fees versus service. There is a fairly wide range.

6. *Don't* forget the radon inspection. This is usually a separate inspection and can run anywhere from $35 to $150. Most relocation companies insist that the home have a separate radon inspection. Bare in mind the magic number in the United States at the time of this printing is 4. The house is not supposed to exceed 4 "picos" (short for picocuries) for it to not be hazardous to your health. Oddly enough, Canada sets the limit at 16 picocuries. Go figure. Anything beyond that raises the question of mitigation. This consists of installing what is actually a fairly simple system of vents and

tubing and sealing off of cracks in the basement. Capping a sump pump can also go a long way to reducing radon on the home. Also, the inspector should not be in the radon mitigation business. That would clearly be a conflict of interest.

7. *Don't* use an inspector who can't do the job right away. There are plenty of them out there, and you shouldn't be allowed to hold up a transaction because you want a specific inspector. Get another one who is equally as qualified to do the job, right now.

8. *Don't* be afraid to ask questions during the actual inspection. That's the perfect time to ask. You are actually helping the inspector do his job better if you ask questions as the process is occurring.

9. *Don't* be surprised if the inspector doesn't put holes in the walls to see what is behind them. Destruction of property is not in the rulebook. In most instances the inspector will be making visual inspections of what he can see. You can see the same things, too. It's just that his expertise helps him or her make more meaningful interpretations. The inspector may not actually go on the roof either. Most inspectors make their observations from the ground. Some use binoculars. Don't be surprised by this either. It's standard procedure.

10. And lastly, *don't* take the inspector's findings as absolute. Remember that you are getting someone else's opinion, nothing more. Granted, you are hoping his opinion will be better than yours, and it should be worth whatever he is charging you. But it is still nothing more than an opinion.

Here's something else to keep in mind. The home inspector should wear only one hat. If he is doubling as an appraiser, he should be giving his opinion as to the *condition* of the house not its *value*. Valuation is what the *appraiser* is concerned with. As paradoxical as it sounds, inspection and appraisal are two different functions and should be kept separate. A frequent problem occurs when FHA (Federal Housing Administration) appraisers do a job and a person subsequently closes on the property and something pops up six months later. One example might be a leaky basement. The purchaser will argue that the appraiser said the house was in good condition, otherwise the bank would not have granted the loan. That's not the point. The appraiser is there to render an opinion on value, not condition.

Now what about buying a property subject to a home inspection? You must know my feelings on this by now. If you are the seller, by all means have someone go through the house with the inspector *before* there is a contract. Don't get entangled in a contract subject to an inspection so that the buyer can come back and renegotiate the deal.

If you are the buyer, it's your call when to do it. You'll have more leverage if you find the seller who will sell it subject to the inspection. As it happens, this is more or less the way it gets done in most markets today. Making it "subject to" is an effort by most real estate communities to make the transaction move ahead. The argument is why should the would-be buyer shell out the money if the seller is not committed to selling it to him in the first place. My argument would be, why should the seller tie up his property for three to five days not knowing if the sale is real or not? Besides, if the buyer is that concerned about the few dollars he has to come up with I have one thing to say: "Hey, that's the cost of doing business."

Okay, so you want to buy it "subject to." Just be careful how the contract is worded. Let me give you two examples that can have a very different result even though the intention is the same. Let's look at the first clause:

Purchaser shall, at his/her own cost and expense,
promptly retain an inspector, contractor or engineer to

inspect the premises and shall receive from said contractor or engineer a report acceptable to purchaser within _____ days of execution of this contract by all parties concerning the condition of the premises. Seller will cooperate with purchaser's inspection in such a fashion as to reasonably requests by purchaser. In the event that said inspection reveals conditions that were unknown to the purchaser at the time of signing the offer to purchase, and that are unacceptable to the purchaser for any reason whatsoever, purchaser shall within 48 hours of receipt, provide seller with a copy of the contractor/engineer's report. Seller, at his/her option, shall agree in writing within 3 business days to make repairs satisfactory to the purchaser *[my emphasis]. In the event that seller does not agree, purchaser and /or seller may cancel said contract in writing. etc.*

Let's look at another way of doing it:

Purchaser shall have the option to have the property inspected and/or tested by an inspector or inspectors of then purchaser's choice at the purchaser's cost and expense. Without the express consent of the seller, no inspection or test shall be conducted which would result in physical damage to the property.

(Right to Cancel Contract) If the results of any inspection are unacceptable to purchaser for any reason whatsoever, purchaser shall notify seller or seller's attorney in writing (the results need not be disclosed) *[my emphasis]. In any case either party may cancel this contract upon written notice to the other party.*

Which clause do you like better? Both are good and are currently in use in Erie County, New York. They are reflective of what a typical inspection clause might look like. The first clause gives the seller the option of fixing the repairs.

The second one states that the buyer can walk if he decides he doesn't like the property because "Venus is in retrograde." That's right, he doesn't have to give a reason. In fact, he can use this clause as an excuse to just change his or her mind. So which one do you like? Want a shock? That's right, I like the second one. If the buyer wants to walk away from the deal, I say "good riddance." I'd rather see that than have the buyer come back and renegotiate the deal to death to have this repair done, and then that repair—and then have to do it over because it's not to his satisfaction. The first clause can be a true nightmare. Many times the repairs get made and the buyer is never satisfied and the deal blows up any way. The heck with all that; I say "fish or cut bait." If you want the house after you've had your team of inspectors go through, great; otherwise, "Sayonara!"

Now here's another sticky point. Let's say the property is inspected and the buyer learns that there is a defect in the property that he doesn't want to deal with, let's say it is a hairline crack in the basement. This might be something hardly worth mentioning. He decides not to buy. Here's the question: Does the seller or the seller's agent have an obligation to disclose this microscopic crack to any subsequent buyer? The answer is absolutely, positively, unequivocally *yes*. Even if the defect is stupid and in their opinion clearly not anything worth mentioning. They have to disclose it, and the next potential purchaser needs to evaluate the merit of the defect in their decision to buy.

Most real estate agents are not in the least bit threatened by home inspectors—if they are good and do their job ethically. The problem is, as I stated earlier, that since it is a totally unregulated segment of the real estate industry, many transactions that should come together don't, because of what I call the Bozo Factor. There are just too many bozos out there claiming to be competent inspectors when clearly they are not. If a transaction dies because of a legitimate objection, then in the long run everyone is better off.

Nobody wants a buyer to buy a house he didn't think he was buying. It's bad business all around.

I happen to have lots of friends who are home inspectors. So while I was formulating my ideas for this book, I asked one of them what his biggest beefs were about his business. I should add that this particular individual is a past president of the National Association of Home Inspectors. He stated that the two things that upset him most are:

1. When the client doesn't want to show up for the inspection, and
2. When they simply don't read the report and they call him up and say, "What about this and what about that," with respect to items that are clearly described in the report.

You know what, that would probably make me crazy too. Remember to work *with* your home inspector rather than against him or her.

Chapter 11

Buying with Nothing Down: It *Can* Be Done

Today's lesson is: How you can buy real estate with nothing down. First, you need an incredibly big Army . . .
—Attila the Hun

uying real estate with nothing down is easy. In fact, in the back of this book I've listed several good titles that can get you started. You've also probably seen many late-night infomercials selling all kinds of tapes and seminars designed to teach you about nothing-down scenarios. Many of these infomercials show people lounging around on beaches and yachts who have managed to build and rebuild their real estate portfolios while doing practically nothing.

This may be a nice fantasy, but it isn't grounded in reality. I don't know whether it was Confucius or John Paul Getty—heck, it might have been yours truly—who first said the immortal words, "From nothing comes nothing." Sure, you can acquire properties for little or no cash down. The cash is the only "nothing" part. There will still be an awful lot of something you have to combine with these kinds of strategies to make the equation work.

The first thing you are going to need is know-how, and the second thing is the ability to make the payments. What many people forget in these nothing-down schemes is the old axiom that says, "You can pay now or you can pay later, but sooner or later, you are going to have to pay." Sometimes buying with nothing down is absolutely, positively *not* the right strategy for the savvy investor. But perhaps this isn't the time to get into my dissertation on deficit spending and about how the government was able to get our national debt into the stratosphere by using such fiscally irresponsible approaches to wealth building. For right now, I'll offer you some sure-fire strategies for procuring real estate with little or no money down.

VA Mortgages

Here's the easiest one. Calling all veterans! That's right. If you are a veteran who has bravely given his or her time to the U.S. armed forces (whether you have risked your life in battle or not), you are in luck. Your veteran's benefits include the ability to go out and purchase a home for nothing down. If you structure the deal right, you can even wind up walking away with a few bucks and the property as well. Remember the caveat though; you still have to make the payments. The larger the amount of the mortgage, the higher your payments. It never ceases to amaze me how banks and lending institutions try to get all of us deeper into debt by allowing us to get in very obviously over our heads with financing payments. But don't worry about the payments just yet; here are some quick guidelines for VA mortgages.

If you are a veteran, the first thing you need to do is contact your local VA administrative office and get a certificate of eligibility. Now the key thing to remember is that the veteran's administration is not going to lend you any money, not one nickel. What they will do is guarantee that if you borrow money through a reputable lending institution (such as a bank), they will guarantee your loan in the unfortunate circumstance that you might be unable to repay that loan (default). Banks will also go one step further. If you have your nifty little certificate in hand, they will extend you the privilege of financing up to $203,000 with absolutely nothing down.

Sound too good to be true? It may be unbelievable, but, in fact, that's the deal in a nutshell. It is truly incredible. The only catch (and it is not a catch, really) is that just like any other loan or mortgage, you are required to show the lender how you are able to repay the debt. If you are gainfully employed and have a track record of repayment (a good credit history, that is) then you're in, and the government will even cut you some slack on the qualifications. Normally banks look for credit ratios of 25%/36% or 28%/38% (income/debt). The VA will let your debt ratio climb to over 40 percent, which I would say is dangerously high, but no matter, they will bend over backwards to give you this deal. All you have to do is ask.

Remember, I said if you structured it right you could even walk away from the table with money. To accomplish that all you have to do is negotiate a few points into the transaction (seller pays) and with nothing down there should be some cash left over for moving expenses. Discuss the best way to structure the transaction with your agent and/or your mortgage rep. They are truly your best friends when it comes to making these kinds of offers. This is when their true value comes into play.

More Nothing-Down Strategies

So what if you're not a veteran? Can you still go with a nothing down strategy? Absolutely! Here's another tactic that works for just about anyone: Find a property that has a high assumable mortgage. Many times motivated sellers will simply want out of a property for many reasons (such as the usual "death, divorce, or transfer"). If their properties happen to have high freely assumable mortgages on them, you can simply acquire the property for a small assumption fee (usually less than $500) and take over the payments. Granted, these properties are harder to find then those in a catalogue of open houses, and finding sellers who are truly highly motivated is a big issue, but such deals are out there if you are willing to look. Oddly enough, your best resource for finding these kinds of purchasing opportunities is, you guessed it, your friendly reliable real estate agent.

What if you find a motivated seller and the property has a high assumable mortgage, but you still need money? Let's use the following example:

Purchase price:	$100,000
Assumable mortgage:	− $80,000
Cash needed:	= $20,000

Do you have to pull your hard-earned cash out of your pocket to make the deal fly? Maybe not. What if the seller really needs to let go of the property? It is conceivable that in this instance the seller might be willing to take back a second mortgage (subordinate to the bank's first) for the difference of $20,000. It is also conceivable that the seller might try to negotiate with you and come out with some cash, perhaps $5,000 or $10,000. You still get to acquire a property with little or "nothing" down. Don't be afraid to negotiate. If you hang in long enough you can find properties and sellers that will be willing to make deals like this. The key will always be motivation. And yes, you will have to look at a lot of properties and make a lot of offers to make the strategy work.

Here's a third no-money-down approach. Suppose you can't find properties that have assumable mortgages. You can always rent to own. Many sellers will be happy to credit some or all of your rent toward the purchase price. Let's say you find a property you like. Rent it for a year and get the seller to credit 100 percent of the rent toward the purchase price. That could end up to equaling a lot of money. Highly motivated sellers are not as loath to go along with this as you might think. The key with this strategy, as with many of the little-or-nothing-down concepts, is that the seller often will be willing to give fabulous terms if you are able to demonstrate the ability to perform (i.e., qualify for a mortgage, etc.) and are willing to pay the *price*. Don't be surprised if the seller wants to negotiate further and credit you with less than 100 percent of the rent. Fifty percent might be more acceptable. But at least you are still using the little-or-nothing-down concept to lower your out-of-pocket cash exposure.

You might instead like strategy four: This one relies on your ability to find someone who owns a property outright. That is to say, they have 100 percent equity. In cases like this, if the seller is motivated you might offer full price and simply say, "You hold the mortgage." When a seller owns a property with no mortgage, he or she has the liberty to play the role of the bank and name his or her own financing terms. If the seller is motivated, many times the potential buyer can ask for extremely favorable terms. This again is presuming that there is no underlying mortgage to pay off at closing. That usually means that the property is less desirable or has some other problem (e.g., a bad location). Sometimes if the seller wants to unload the house, he would rather have payments instead of dealing with the everyday grind of managing an unwanted property. Sometimes it works out well for both parties where one party trades equity for paper. You have to find the property first, the qualified seller second, and then you have to sell your proposal. If he listens to you for even a second, there is a distinct possibility you may have found a match and be closer to a deal that you may suspect.

Let's go for the fifth option: trading sweat equity. You might post a performance bond and work your way into ownership of a property. A performance bond is nothing more than a formal agreement in writing between the parties that one will perform a service for another with specific consequences if they do not comply. Frequently, working people with skills in certain trades (e.g., plumbing, electrical, etc.) can negotiate an exchange for service and literally buy a position for partial or full equity by offering their labor in place of actual dollars. The practice is much more common than you might think. A performance bond, like a mortgage, merely insures that you are, in fact, going to do what you say you are going to do.

"To bifurcate or not to bifurcate, that is the question." Here's a fairly common approach. Find a property. Arrange for financing and then simply ask the seller to hold a second mortgage that absorbs what you would have been using as your total down payment. Bifurcation simply implies that there is more than one purchase money mortgage in place to affect a transfer, with one subordinated to the other. Let's look at a scenario:

Selling price:	$100,000
First mortgage:	$80,000
Second mortgage:	$20,000
Cash required:	$0

One key issue is that you have to find a seller who is willing to risk the possibility that he may get stiffed on the remaining $20,000. That may not be as difficult as you think. It has to do with the old risk/reward ratio. He will be getting 80 percent up front, right? This would be pretty decent odds for most gamblers. And, of course, the seller can always chase you and start a foreclosure action, in the unfortunate case that you choose to default.

The second point you need to bear in mind is very important. Depending on the way you structure the transaction, it might not be even doable in the first place, and it could run you into legal problems. Bifurcation used to be a very common business practice in the '80s. It also in great part contributed to the S&L collapses in that decade.

At that time, many properties were being sold without the purchaser having any equity. In other words, he put no money on the table at all. It was all paper. There were maximum loan amounts being underwritten by the lender, and the equity that was supposed to exist was, in actuality, simple paper in the form of a smaller second mortgage. When the crunch hit, and property values dropped, there were countless numbers of portfolios that were chock-filled with properties that not only didn't have any equity but were in fact worth considerably less that the face value of the mortgages.

Many investors who found themselves in the position of no longer being able to make the payments on these upside-down properties simply threw up their hands and told the banks to come and foreclose. For this reason, it is not unusual for lenders to establish certain safeguards to prevent this. What lenders typically do today is simply inform you up front that you cannot borrow the down payment. They may say that you cannot seek secondary financing. They may even ask you to sign an affidavit under the penalty of perjury stating that at the time of closing there is no secondary financing in place. Shrewd purchasers have found a way around this by establishing a double-closing strategy. They take out a purchase money mortgage on a property and sign an affidavit stating that no secondary financing exists at the time of closing. They then close on the property and a day or two later they file a second mortgage. Remember, the affidavit was correctly worded to the purchaser's advantage because it stated that the secondary financing did not exist at the time of closing. It came into existence just *after* closing.

Many lenders have gotten wise to this and have placed an additional safeguard on their lending guidelines. They may make the loan "callable" should the purchaser ever place subordinate financing on the property anytime during the time the first mortgage exists. Simply put, when a loan is callable, it means that the entire balance of the loan is now due. The lender is calling it in.

More Strategies for Little or No Money Down

Seven is a lucky number. So let's look at a seventh way to get you some properties with little or no equity. Remember these three letters: REO. They stand for Real Estate Owned. These are properties that banks and other lending institutions have simply taken back (foreclosed) and now find themselves proudly owning. You would be amazed at how many properties banks own.

Here's a simple thing to bear in mind when you approach a bank's "salvage department." (Most banks have these separate departments where their inventory of foreclosed properties are kept.) Banks are not in the real estate business; they are in the lending business. They do not want to be in the real estate business. They are no good at the real estate business. They do not want to own and continue to maintain these properties. Their product is money, not real estate. Real estate is just one vehicle they use to make money. Consumer loans might be another.

Most often banks would *love* to turn these liabilities into assets by getting them off their books and into someone else's hands. They would much rather hold a large mortgage (even 100 percent) and be getting those big payments with all that nice interest. It doesn't make a lot of sense for them to keep forking out cash for upkeep and taxes.

If you want to find some great deals that you can pick and choose from, contact lenders and ask about REO properties. I recently acquired an account with Ford Credit Corporation. They were up to their eyebrows in inventory.

They were offering 100 percent financing at competitive rates with a quick qualification procedure. (The paperwork was limited, because they were going to keep the loans in their own portfolios rather that trying to resell them on the secondary market.) Ford Credit took it one step further and offered to pay the purchaser's closing costs. Are you getting a sense that they wanted to get rid of some properties?

Don't be afraid to ask about REOs. Perhaps I should say *shop* for REOs. You will find bargains you could not even begin to know existed. Check with large real estate firms, too. Most of them have properties that fall into this category, and nothing would delight them more than to unload a few. They make a profit from these in ways you can't imagine. How, you ask?

Many times large real estate firms have a separate subsidiary lending institution affiliated with them. They get to underwrite the mortgages. If you buy, and then later upgrade the property, there is a good possibility they will get your business on the resale, either on the list side or the sale side, or, if they really get lucky, on both sides. From a long-range perspective, properties that get upgraded increase the valuations of neighboring properties that may already be on the market. It's good business anyway you slice it. But the key is that they have to get them out of their inventory and turn them back into assets. These are assets that become yours, if you have the mind and the nerve to tackle them.

Strategy eight is *equity sharing*. That's right, you can always take in a partner. He or she posts the money (cash up front); you post the "know-how" and/or the credit worthiness. Either way you can gain access to a property without putting up the cash.

Strategy nine: You can always "trade stuff." People often have assets other than cash that are equally desirable. Some examples include: boats, cars, jewels, expertise in a particular field, travel benefits, etc. These hard and soft assets can be traded for equity positions in real estate. One man's trash is another man's treasure, and trading trash for treasure is a sure way to increase your wealth. Look around you and see what things you have that can be traded (things that are of value that you may not want). You may be sitting on a potential gold mine. One thing that is frequently traded is property management skills. You put up the time, talent, and effort, and many times investors are willing to cut you in for a piece of the equity.

Strategy ten: Special finance deals offered through mortgage brokers. Many lenders periodically carry "special" deals in an effort to have people purchase properties in certain target areas or in a specific income bracket. One such program is called the "community buyers program"; it offers a 3-percent-down deal that will even let you take the 3 percent and finance that further with an unsecured note.

For these types of programs, you either need the savvy partnership of a good broker or a good mortgage rep. Sit down with these folks and ask them. Another thing that these programs have in common is that, as a rule, the purchaser needs to have relatively pristine credit. That would stand to reason, since the lender is willing to extend you that much leverage. If you don't get the answers you want, ask other Realtors and other mortgage bankers. These programs can be found all over the country, but you have to ask and you have to be willing to submit to the "trial by paper." Since these programs are mostly underwritten by government agencies, there is a mountain of paperwork. But they are well worth it if you don't have to come up with a lot of hard-earned cash.

Are there more ways for you to get into the real estate game without playing with your own chips? Sure there are. But these ten should give you a good starting point. Ten ways to get you going if you are daring and if you remember what I warned you about earlier. *You have to be able to make the payments.* If you can't, the entire strategy of buying with little or no money down will be for naught.

One other thing worth mentioning: Beware of those closing costs. Sometimes you can get in for little or nothing down, but you still have closing costs. Depending on where you live, they can run you as high as 8 percent of the purchase price, if you take into consideration those nasty little fees called prepayables or escrows. Don't be so slick as to negotiate one of these deals only to come up short at the closing table because you failed to take into account those fees that brokers like to call "soft costs." Soft costs can be a real killer. Again, it's one more reason to make the real estate broker your best friend in the world. Getting him or her involved in the process can sometimes provide you with opportunities to get around some of those soft costs, or even get some of them waived in certain instances.

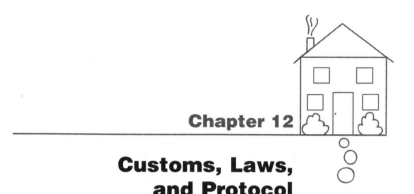

Chapter 12

Customs, Laws, and Protocol

I don't think we're in Kansas anymore, Toto.
—Dorothy, in *The Wizard of Oz*

art of the problem with living in the United States is that the fifty little sovereignties involved are not very, how shall I say, *united*. Not only do we have to contend with having fifty separate governing bodies and Departments of State, but procedures can vary widely within each state itself. That's right. Within most states there is a broad range of inconsistencies in real estate practice. In New York, for example, with more than twenty counties, a real estate transaction varies significantly from county to county. Moreover, when you look at the way business is done upstate as opposed to downstate, you really begin to scratch your head.

What is even more preposterous is the sometimes widely divergent practices within the boundaries of a single municipality! The best example of this is New York City itself. New York City is made up of five boroughs, Manhattan being only one of them (that's the Big Apple itself, or what people who live in the other boroughs refer to as "the City"). As it turns out, businesses in the outer boroughs utilize a system similar to that used in many other markets; this is known as the Multiple Listing Service. The MLS allows brokers to cooperate and share information so that, theoretically, it makes it easier for the consumer to look at a broader range of properties. It also, by definition, rewards its participating members with a unilateral agreement of cooperation (sometimes referred to as "sub-agency"), and it makes mutual compensation much easier.

In Manhattan and in most of downtown Brooklyn the MLS is virtually ignored. Basically, if you want to shop for properties you are obligated to go from broker to broker. In the absence of this system, brokers have to do much more negotiating when it comes to the small matter of getting paid. (By the way, a good question to ask *any* broker you are considering working with is, "Exactly how is it that you get paid?" This question may appear stupid, but it will show any agent that you are a savvy would-be client. He will respect you for asking, because it puts the question of compensation and agency right on the table from the get-go.)

You are probably thinking, "Hey, all I wanted to do was buy a house." You should realize, though, that there might be all sorts of behind-the-scenes dealing that you may be totally unaware of in cities like this. A difference in listing services is only one example of how business procedure will vary with the geography.

How properties are shown varies widely as well. In some parts of the country you will observe widespread use of lock boxes. These boxes, which hang from the front or back door of a given property, have the key to the premises inside them. An agent will have the combination to the box and will gain access to the premises. These old-style combination lock boxes are thankfully becoming harder to find, because agents often forget to give them a new code when they come from the factory. This could present a considerable security risk for many sellers.

Fortunately, the "electronic" boxes that are now in vogue greatly enhance security for the homeowner as well as for the agent. Each agent carries a battery-operated keypad that attaches itself to the box. The agent puts in his or her personal code and—presto!—it opens. The box will also record the access code and the time of the showing. This way, the listing office knows exactly who has gained admission to the home and when. The advantages of the technologically improved lock box are clear.

In many areas, agents still show properties the old-fashioned way and either wait for the homeowner to be home or use courtesy keys that are supposed to be locked up in their offices when not in use. Do you want to hear something really scary? You would be absolutely amazed how carelessly real estate offices take care of their keys. I know of one office where all of the keys for the available homes are laid out on a desk, with the addresses clearly printed on each and every one. If a burglar ever broke into that office, he would have clear access to scores of very attractive homes simply by using the key to the front door. If you are thinking of listing your home with a Realtor, be sure to ask them how they handle the key situation in their office.

Here's another aspect of the process of showing houses to consider: Who calls whom to register the appointments? Many markets do not allow the agent to just use the lock box. The appointment must first be registered. Some agents are required to call the listing office to register the showing. Other areas allow the agent to call the homeowner directly. One thing is for certain: If you want to drive an agent completely crazy, ask her to set up a series of appointments to look at various homes and then cancel at the last minute for some unlikely excuse.

The title of this chapter mentions the word *protocol*. Simply not showing up for an arranged appointment is very much frowned upon in any jurisdiction. In some cases, homeowners have the right to be notified that you are coming so they can make arrangements to be out of the house. Being a "no show" really burns the agent and many times seriously frosts the homeowner as well. Really good agents will have a heart-to-heart talk with you if you cancel on them more than once. If you do it twice and they don't say something, they are either brain dead or have no concept of self-worth. An agent's time is very valuable; she likes to work by appointment and she likes to stick to a schedule. For agents, time is definitely money, and they don't take kindly to folks who are cavalier about wasting their time.

The Protocol of Contracts

Contracts and what's in them are another part of the transaction that can vary like the proverbial snowflake. They can be as simple as a "binder," which is nothing more than a one-page document that shows receipt of a small initial deposit. They might be more complex with documents running into ten, twenty, thirty pages, or more. The person who can provide the best insight into what kind of sales contract you should be using is the agent.

In Erie County, New York, where I currently practice, the contract has been significantly changed and "updated" at least three times in the last decade. Each time, the contract was changed to make it simpler and more user-friendly. Each time, it was "improved" to make it better for the consumer. In the process, it changed from a one-page contract to a four-page contract, and currently it rolls off the presses at seven pages, not including "riders." With each revision the cost of doing business rises. And, you guessed it, longer contracts entail more legal fees. Something else to consider is the probability of litigation increasing as well. So much for simplifying! Who will steer you through the maze and tell you what the contract will look like and how it should proceed in your area? That's right, your agent.

Are you buying a home contingent on the sale of another

home—such as a current residence? In one part of the country that may be business as usual while in another area they will look at you as if you were from another planet. What's the practice in your area? You have to ask. Right now in areas of the Silicon Valley if you even suggested a contingent sale it would warrant you a trip to a sanitarium. Conversely, in most rural parts of the country it is standard practice. And, as we may have mentioned before, for properties that are listed with relocation companies you can pretty much bet on forgetting about contingencies.

Lending policies are a separate category. They vary not just from place to place, and state to state, but from moment to moment. Change is so relentless that if you don't have a good mortgage banker on your team, wherever you are, you may as well just toss out this entire book and every other piece of common sense you might have acquired up to this point. Rates are moving, ratios are adjusting, Loans to Value (a.k.a. LTVs) are being modified faster than you can imagine. But that's just the half of it. The paper requests and the endless faxes with account numbers and verifications on top of verifications are truly what will make you say to yourself, "What the heck is going on? Can I get a little help here?"

Closing anyone? In states where there are attorneys carrying the ball, closings can take on entirely different interpretations when it comes to time. Title states are much simpler and faster, with settlement usually occurring between two weeks and thirty days. That's how it should be, barring unforeseen circumstances. When you have three lawyers working (each with a separate agenda), you are looking at ninety-day turnarounds without batting an eyelash.

In my firm right now we are averaging eighty-three days from contract to closing. That is taking into consideration that that figure is down from eighty-seven days in the previous year. We did in excess of 6,000 closings in each year, with sales totaling around three-quarters of a billion, so the "average" figure is pretty reliable. We might as well tell our clients "forever" when they ask us how long it takes to close. Why it has to take that long is one of the great crimes that has been perpetrated on the consumer and goes well beyond the scope of this chapter. Your agent will keep you apprised as to what you should expect in your neck of the woods.

Can the agent do anything to speed the process along? The answer is yes and no. A good agent can establish a sense of urgency with all the players in the deal. He or she can direct you to the right mortgage lender who can "process" the loan faster and get it to pass underwriting more quickly. A good agent may have an in-house mortgage lender who does a high volume of business with lots of lenders. Those types of relationships enable the agent to call in a favor more readily or ask to have the file updated and reviewed. All of these approaches are both legitimate and legal. High-volume customers can simply ask that their file get placed on the top of the pile. That's all. When working with your agent, you might ask if he has the kind of relationship with a lender that will get you the best rate and fastest approval. Regardless of what market you're in, that's a fair and valid question and will further distinguish you as a savvy client.

The actual place where you close can be any of a number of places. Depending on where you are in the country, the most typical answers might be: at the bank, at a lawyer's office, at the title company, or maybe even right at the county hall. This last location is for the total convenience of "closers" and attorneys so that they can save themselves a trip down to the county hall to record the documents. If you would prefer to make it more convenient for yourself, you can always speak up and ask or even insist that the closing occur where you want it to be. They may or may not charge you for this change in venue. Check with your agent and/or attorney.

The key thing to remember about anything in this chapter is "When in Rome, do as the Romans do." This is a good axiom. But suppose you don't want to eat spaghetti on this particular day? Will it disrupt everyone else's meal? The things you ask for may be totally insignificant in and of themselves. They can also be beyond major in their underlying ramifications. You need to first ask what is appropriate. Then you can get into questions like, "Well, what would happen if we did it *this* way?" If you meet resistance, you cannot just sit idly back, however. You must immediately follow up with a polite, "And why is that?"

Property Condition Disclosures

What about property condition disclosures? They can vary tremendously. In about thirty-six of the fifty states there is currently a legal requirement that the seller make a full written property condition disclosure. The remaining states are unconcerned with this, or so it would appear. Perhaps they have either not gotten around to addressing the issue or are unresolved as to whom such disclosures protect. As it happens, the National Association of Realtors recommends a written disclosure for all of its members.

In spite of the fact that New York State did not require the use of a disclosure for the longest time, my firm has used one for years. The largest broker in the state (a nearby competitor) did not. Their justification for not using a written property disclosure is that they felt it provided one more document that could lead to possible litigation. The National Association of Realtors' stance on this is that in all states—and that's *all* states—that have enacted laws mandating written condition disclosure, the incidence of lawsuit because of undisclosed property conditions dropped dramatically. My own firm's error and omissions rates would support this claim.

Common sense would tell you that this is a good thing. The homeowner is telling you exactly what he knows to be the truth. If he is lying, he is at risk for libel or fraudulent representation. If he honestly doesn't know, you have a duty to discover those facts for yourself. Isn't that why God made home inspectors? So ask your agent if there is a written property disclosure, and if yours is a state that requires one. If there isn't one, ask if the seller will agree to supply you with one anyway.

In my opinion, there really is no down side for the seller to supply you with one, if he is telling the truth. Besides, you will only find out the truth for yourself later anyway. I don't believe it will kill a deal. It may make you decide not to purchase, but you might have decided that anyway when you learned what was in the inspection report. Incidentally, in March 2002, the state of New York finally got around to mandating written property disclosure. In the process, they put a little extra spin on it. Should the seller fail to supply a written disclosure to the purchaser prior to the signing of the contract, there is an automatic credit of $500 awarded to the purchaser.

Putting Up Some Cash

The way that offers are conveyed also varies with the local customs. Take *earnest money*, for example. Simply put, earnest money is any token amount that is used as an initial deposit in order to establish that the prospective buyer is acting in "earnest" or good faith. What's the right amount? It depends on where you are. In some places it might be presumed that a minimum 10 percent is necessary. In other places you might get by with as little as $100. It is not the laws that dictate these amounts. It is the local customs and the swiftness of the market. However, regardless of where you are, some token amount is in order.

As you approach the offer stage, the agent you are working with might even ask, "So what can you give me to get the ball rolling?" Your response should always be, "As little as possible." Nevertheless, you will be well advised to listen carefully and follow your own agent's advice. Don't be surprised, by the way, if she recommends more than you might expect. She is interested in helping you show your good faith. The more money you initially put up, the greater the sense of good faith you convey. Incidentally, certain brokers in New York City will convey an offer on a property over the phone without any good faith deposit at all. It's odd, but it's done. As you might imagine, many of these offers are deemed to be less than credible. After all, there is no stake in the game. No one will take you that seriously when you haven't yet put your money where your mouth is.

After the good faith deposit is agreed upon, the offer can get conveyed any number of ways, according to custom. It might be done most expeditiously over the phone, with all counteroffers conveyed the same way. It might be transmitted via fax or the U.S. mail. It might be conveyed by the agents, with a face-to-face dialogue, or with only the seller present. The offer might also simply be conveyed to a third party who works in a relocation department, presuming that there was a corporate buy-out.

It might be what they call a sit-down contract. That is where an interested buyer comes in and sits down with all the agents involved and the seller as well, and they negotiate the dickens out of everything, eyeball to eyeball. These kinds of peace talk negotiations can sometimes go on for hours and become bloody. The good news is they frequently result in a great deal for everyone with all the minor terms worked out up front. For all of the initial aggravation, this type of contract can work out quite well.

Recently, one of my agents put the question to me: "Don't I have the right to directly present my buyer's offer to the seller in person? It's a full-price cash offer, by the way." Now you have to realize I live in one of those places where the custom is (as archaic as this sounds) that you present offers to the listing agent and the seller in person. It was obvious to me that the agent working with the buyer was a major control freak and the motive for the question needed some further exploration.

"What's the problem here?" I asked. "If it is a full-price cash offer and you're telling me that there are no other offers, then phone it in and be done with it. What purpose could it possibly have for you to run clear across town, just so that you can show the agent how smug you really can be?"

"Well, I think she (the other agent) is trying to give me the runaround."

"Okay, here's the deal," I explained. "It is certainly within the province of your buyer to insist that the offer is being made subject to his agent conveying the offer in person. He can certainly do that. That's his call, not yours. Why he would feel it necessary is certainly a question I would need squarely resolved before I would put that into a contract. If the seller tells you, listen, I don't want to be bothered with this face-to-face nonsense, just tell my agent and have her call me, what are you going to do? Cancel the deal because of some silly imagined protocol issue?" I don't think so.

In any event, that's what I told her. She did as I suggested, and she realized after my mini-dissertation that I was right. I mean, come on people, we're talking full price cash!

Always remember that customs and protocol are very nice, and it's nice to be polite. Moreover, it is always terrific to do things as the "Romans" do when and where it is appropriate. Just be clear as to what the customs are, and what the proper protocol is, and recognize you can vary from them a little without starting a feud.

Law Versus Protocol

Protocol may be important, but laws are laws, and you want to make damned certain that you have the right advice in respect to them. You could find yourself in serious trouble if you decide to "bend" one of them in your zeal to get a deal expedited. So be careful, and just don't be too aggressive in attempting to get the best end of the deal. Ask questions. Talk to your agent and your legal representative. Follow their suggestions. They might just know what they are talking about, and they may even save you some time, trouble, and aggravation. The best part is, they might just save you some money, too. And remember that abnormality might just be the norm in your locality.

Exam Time

By this point you should be much more savvy about real estate tricks of the trade. Remember the quiz in Chapter 2? How many of the questions can you answer now? Test your knowledge—or your agent's—against the answers provided.

1. Suppose the buyer is scheduled to bring in a second deposit after the binder or earnest money deposit has been collected, and he simply forgets to show up with the money. Is the deal dead?

That depends. Your deal isn't necessarily dead, but you need to ask to determine why the buyer hasn't shown up with the second check. Did he simply forget (possible, but a long shot)? Is he transferring money from one account to another? Has he had second thoughts as to the problems that popped up in the home inspection? Is he simply suffering from buyer's remorse in the truest sense of the word? No, I would say that the deal is not dead. It would be more accurate to say that your deal is dying and in any event the patient isn't looking all that well. There is still room for a tremendous recovery provided immediate action or resuscitation takes place.

2. How much time do you allow for the attorney to chase the buyer for the additional funds? Or is that the agent's job?

How much time you allow depends on your threshold for pain and how much additional interest has been shown in the property. Let's presume that things are at a standstill and no one else is barking up your tree. It's about that time the buyer decides to get weird on you. The agent should get right on the case, and your attitude should be, "What the heck is going on here?" Your attorney should be brought into the act immediately. The more pressure you can bring in at this point, the better. You need to resolve right away if the buyer is alive or not so you can get on with the constructive marketing of the property. You don't want to have to sell the property to someone else subject to the release of a prior contract. It just gets too murky and problematical. Finish the initial play and follow it to whatever resolution you can. Then get on with life and your next transaction.

3. Whose escrow account should these moneys be deposited into: the seller's attorney, the listing agent, or an escrow agent?

Whose escrow account? Generally, custom will decide this. The key issue is that the money should be held in a third party's hands (separate account). It should not be in the buyer's account or the seller's account. Many times the broker for the seller holds the escrow money and he becomes, or I should say *the firm* becomes, the escrow agent. Sometimes the attorney for the seller becomes the escrow agent. Sometimes title companies and escrow agents are actually named. I did have an unusual sale once where the buyer was an attorney and he wanted to hold his own escrow deposit. I said to him, "Now, let me get this straight, you want to buy this house, and YOU want to hold your own down payment?" "That's right," he said. "I've been burned before and have had to wait too long to get my money back on other deals, and I'm holding the down payment or I am not buying. Take it or leave it."

Common sense would tell anyone that a third, neutral party should hold any and all escrow deposits. But this is how I handled it. First of all, remember I had a fiduciary obligation (to obey, use reasonable care, etc.) to the seller, so I told him what the would-be purchaser wanted to do. I explained to him that this was indeed highly unusual and that, in fact, this would be a first in my experience. It wasn't illegal; it was just kind of bizarre. As long as he understood that this was far from standard operating procedure, it was his decision. Another factor was that this property had had two deals go down the toilet already, and the seller was beyond motivated to unload the place. Based on these additional circumstances, the seller said, "What the hell, I'm no worse off now than if I don't go along with it, right?"

It turned out to be the easiest transaction I ever had, and the deal closed like clockwork. You see, I also knew something else. Because the buyer was an attorney, he had to be held to a higher standard than you or I would be, considering that he was an officer of the court with a greater obligation to follow professional ethics. If he decided to get cute at the last minute, he could be brought before his local bar association and censured. In this case, given the unusual set of facts leading to the decision to move forward, the risks seemed minimal and more than worth the gamble.

4. Does the account draw interest, and if so, who is entitled to that interest?

Interest is not automatic. It is up to the buyer to ask, or even insist, that the escrow deposit be held in an interest bearing account. Some agents or companies will say to you that their company policy is such that there is a minimum amount required before they will place it in an account. However, the law provides that it must be a separate account. It does not have to be interest bearing, but it must be a separate account.

Many times the agency would rather not place the escrow into an interest-bearing account because there is added paperwork as well as additional fees that they have to incur. Under the law, they are permitted to pass them on to you. You need to determine how much interest you will in fact earn in this account and determine whether or not it is worth it. The interest is yours (if you are the buyer) and is paid to you as a part of the closing disbursements. Can the escrow agent elect on his own to not place it in an interest bearing account? It is not his prerogative to do so. But remember; you have to ask because it is not automatic.

5. Suppose the property is appraised for less than the contract sales price? Is the deal dead? Does the offer get renegotiated? Does the buyer simply call it a day and get his money back?

Yes, yes, yes, and yes to the last question if that's what the buyer wants. When a person elects to buy a property, subject to a mortgage being obtained from a reputable lending institution, he is doing so subject to that institution's terms. One of their conditions is that their interest is protected by a good-faith, independent "guesstimate" of value. This is what we know as an appraisal. If the property isn't appraised, the buyer often feels he overpaid and would like to renegotiate the deal. He can do this if in fact he still wants to go through with the transaction. One thing is certain: Something will have to give to keep the transaction afloat.

Another possibility is to ask for a second appraisal. This is the buyer's prerogative. The seller can't say, "Let me bring in my appraiser, he'll do a better job." Even if he could, you need to remember that it is the buyer's prerogative, not the seller's, to ask for the second appraisal. He might ask the seller to pay for it, since it seems like now the seller has an interest in making sure the property appraises "up to the market." A third possibility is that the buyer takes some extra money out of his pocket to make up for the shortfall of the banks LTV (loan to value). Or maybe the buyer and seller agree to split the difference to make the deal work.

6. Can you appeal an appraisal?

Yes, absolutely. As I mentioned in the answer to question 5, an appraisal can be appealed—by the buyer. Or more specifically, the bank's client (the buyer) can appeal the appraisal if he still wants to go through with the sale. Typically, what will happen is the agent working with the buyer will ask what the buyer wants to do. Nine times out of ten, the buyer will say, "Well, of course I still want to buy the house." The agent at that point, in an effort to save the deal, will look for serious comparable properties ("comps"—similar properties, in similar locations, that have closed within the last six months).

If there is no question that the subject property is well worth the price, based on these comps, the buyer's agent will suggest a second appraisal. He may, as his first line of attack, at least discuss what comps the original appraiser used. He will try to refrain from calling the appraiser an idiot to his face. But let's face it. The appraisal process is not an exact art. It is an opinion. Sometimes the appraiser's opinion does not jibe with the market or with the desires of a willing buyer and a willing seller.

7. If the appraisal is just an opinion of value, who gets to decide if the appraiser is right or wrong?

Who decides if an appraiser is right or wrong? The buyer does. Even if the seller is right, the buyer gets the ultimate say. If the buyer doesn't want to buy, based on the appraiser's opinion, he doesn't buy unless he gets the house for the right renegotiated price or he gets an acceptable second (or third) appraisal. In a sense, the appraiser actually is always right, because, you see, everyone is still entitled to his or her opinion.

8. **Suppose the buyer doesn't get his mortgage commitment in time, should the seller give him additional time? How much time is reasonable?**

Didn't get the mortgage commitment on time? What to do? The first thing that the seller, the buyer, and the agents will want to resolve in their respective minds is *why*. Did the bank need more time to complete the underwriting process? Did the buyer drag his or her heels and not "deliver" the documentation to the loan processor in time? Are the banks hopelessly behind because of a flood of refinancing? Is it as simple a glitch as the underwriter waiting for a verification of employment? You'd be amazed how often this comes up. Does the buyer not want to buy, and if so, has he deliberately dragged his heels? You want to know about these things, and sooner is much better than later.

Does the seller give an extension? Yes, if there is light at the end of the tunnel. How much of an extension should he grant? It could be an additional two weeks or perhaps thirty days. You need some direction from the loan officer and the agents on this issue. Perhaps the seller chooses not to extend because he thinks that there is another more tangible buyer who is willing to step up to the plate. There are lots of ifs and lots of questions. Ninety-nine percent of mortgage extension requests are granted, presuming the answers are satisfactory on all the issues we have just raised here.

9. **If the buyer has been prequalified for a loan, is it possible for him to, in fact, get turned down for the loan after he applies?**

Oh yes! Prequalified does not mean preapproved. Buyers get turned down for loans all the time after they have been prequalified. Prequalified can mean a simple guess, based on income-to-debt ratio. Many times a prequalification is done without running a credit check. A person can have the greatest income in the world and horrific credit.

10. Can a buyer lose a commitment after a bank has issued one?

Yes! This is something else to bear in mind. Even if the buyer is preapproved, and, in fact, obtains a letter of commitment, he can lose his commitment if his status changes. If he loses his job two days before closing, he could get his commitment pulled. This can also happen if the backup house that supposedly was sold suddenly doesn't close. What if a spouse loses a job? What if the buyer decides to run out and buy a car prior to closing (thus altering the debt ratio and kicking out the deal)? All of this and more happens more times then you can imagine, and the seller is left holding the bag (house).

11. What if the buyer refuses to close on the date specified?

If the buyer refuses to close on time, you could have a major problem on your hands. Obviously, the first thing that needs to be established is what's going on. Usually the parties in question will have some inkling that something is amiss before the actual day of closing. It may be a simple error in communication. It may be that the buyer has had some strong misgivings and has decided to get out of the deal. If the buyer refuses to close, some sort of settlement will be offered. Or perhaps, the seller will simply sue, after a last-ditch effort of declaring "time is of the essence."

12. What does "time is of the essence" really mean? When should a buyer or a seller be concerned if they see that phrase in a contract?

Serious business, that's what it means. In the previous example, it means that one party, in this case the seller, has decided to force the issue of closing. A specific time is set. As we see here, if the buyer continues to ignore the specific time for closing, all sorts of legal action can subsequently take place. Sometimes this clause is put into a contract right upfront. It can be enforced against either the seller or the buyer depending on the way it is worded.

This clause is of such a serious nature and can have such broad sweeping consequences that it should never be entered casually. An attorney should always be consulted when you see this definite red flag in a contract.

13. If there is substantial damage to a property prior to a sale, what happens to the sale? Is the contract still valid?

The contract is still valid. The buyer, however, may have reasonable cause to get out of the contract. It is up to the buyer to direct the outcome. Hopefully, the seller will have insurance and can return the property back to the condition it was when the contract was first written. I know of many a case where there was fire or flood damage, and the seller's insurance claim actually resulted in fixing the property to a point that it was in significantly better condition than when the buyer originally bought the premises. If there is no way to return the property to the original condition, the buyer has the option of renegotiating for a lower price or saying, "Happy trails."

14. Either the buyer or the seller dies prior to closing or settlement. What happens?

One of two things can happen: Either the deal folds or the estates can choose to close on the transaction. It is easier for the buyer to get the estate of the seller to close rather than the reverse, by the way.

15. After closing, the purchaser (now the owner) discovers a serious structural defect that he is convinced the seller must have known about, but did not in fact disclose. What are the remedies?

Oh boy! If what we are thinking here actually occurred, the seller is in serious trouble. As we stated in an earlier chapter, the seller has an obligation in all states to disclose any known hidden defects. He obviously can be sued for the cost of the repair. In addition, there could be civil and criminal charges preferred if the fraud is determined to be willful as well as deceitful. The first call goes to your agent, to see if it can be addressed at that level. The second goes to the seller, directly by you, to see if the two of you can come to a reasonable adjustment. The third goes to your attorney, who goes for the jugular.

16. The purchaser can't close on the property because of some serious personal circumstances. Is there a way to legally extricate him from the sale?

Am I even hearing this question? This is a question that a Realtor cannot and should not answer. Let me tell you why. For a licensed real estate agent to give advice on this to either party is to do what is known as "inducing breach of contract." If that sounds serious, it is. All sorts of bad things can happen to an agent who attempts to do this.

But can we talk here, just for a minute? It is difficult for me to imagine that there is not an attorney worth his or her salt who could not find some sort of a legal loophole for either principal if the task was laid before him. Should the question ever be posed to a Realtor or an agent, however, the response should always be the same. They should say words to the effect, "What you're asking me presents me with a serious ethical compromise. If you are looking to do this, please discuss it with your attorney, so that you might better understand the possible consequences of your action, and all its legal ramifications." In other words, "You'd better call your lawyer, buddy."

Now, no doubt, some readers out there are saying to themselves, "Wait a minute, if the buyer wants to get out of the deal, all he needs to do is call his loan rep and ask them to kill the deal based on the financing qualifications." It's true this could provide him with a nice little legal loophole and a very viable way out. There is only one problem. It goes to the issue of good faith. Clearly, the buyer is not acting in good faith. Moreover, they could be asking the loan rep to commit a fraudulent action here as well, which could compromise him legally as well. The tough part about this play is that when push comes to shove, the issue and the action must be proven. I call this the "you gotta catch me" theory of real estate. It is a very unscrupulous thing to do to anybody and one of the dirtier tricks out there.

17. Title problems become obvious prior to closing. What happens? Whose problem is it?

So you've got title problems? Now everyone has a problem. This is, of course, presuming that the parties both want the transaction to proceed along smoothly. If you are a principal, you need to review the Contract of Sale. There will hopefully be a paragraph that indicates what "Remedies" are allowed in a title dispute. It is not such an unusual occurrence. Generally speaking, most contracts call for the conveyance of "good and marketable title" free of clouds and encumbrances. If a claim is made against title or there are some unresolved issues bringing the true nature of the seller's title into question, many contracts call for the ability of the seller to issue what is known as "insurable title."

I recently purchased a property that had an unresolved boundary dispute. The question came up with respect to a survey that described a certain portion of the property—about twenty feet—that was in dispute. One survey clearly showed it on the seller's land. The other showed it to be on the neighboring property. The decision was made to grant insurable title. In essence, the seller found an insurance (title) company that was going to take his wager that the property was in fact rightfully his. They were willing to accept his payment (the premium), in view of the fact that title had been passed twice before in the last twenty years. It also had been insured twice before to boot.

Everyone was betting that if someone else was willing to take the risk, there wasn't much risk involved in the first place. Now here's something to remember. If the seller could not have gotten title insurance, I would not have been able to get a mortgage on the property. Good (or insurable) title is almost always a condition the bank will insist upon. In that case, the only way I would have been able to purchase the property would have been to go cash or owner-hold. That is further presuming that I did not care to make an issue over the unresolved title dispute. For me, these would have been three nearly impossible "ifs." So to wrap up this question, it is up to the seller to resolve the title issue. If he can't, the buyer can get out of the deal.

18. You discover the fence separating the property is ten feet on the neighbor's adjoining yard. What to do?
Have you ever heard the expression, "Good fences make good neighbors"? Generally speaking, this is true. Sometimes, though, it makes for a one hell of a boundary dispute. You discover that your neighbor's fence encroaches ten feet on your property. Want to hear something scary? The neighbor may be able to claim that ten feet as rightfully *his* property. He may be able to make this claim in an action that is entitled "adverse possession." If your neighbor has been using that property for at least ten years, and treating it as his own, it could be ruled in a court of law that it in fact now is his. Forget what your survey may say. Here is the stipulation. If he has been using the land openly, deliberately, and notoriously for the specified period of time, wham, it's his. So if you knew the fence was on your property, and you waved to him for ten years, and watched him cut the grass each year, and he waved backed to you (that's the notorious part), congratulations. You just legally allowed your neighbor to seize your land. You would be surprised how often this comes up, and not just in places like the Wild West, where range wars were commonplace.

That's why you want to have an up-to-date, accurate survey. It is also why you want to very politely, yet firmly, tell your neighbor, "Excuse me, I don't mean to be a pain, but I think your fence is on my property. You see, I was checking my survey. And I'm sure there must be some sort of error here. And I don't want to sound like a nasty neighbor, because I just hate it when you read about neighbors having petty squabbles about silly little things like this. So that's why, well, I don't know how to really say this, but could you move it, NOW!"

19. The assumable mortgage on the property turns out to be not assumable. What can be done to save the deal?

Assumable mortgage—now you see it, now you don't. The only way to definitively respond to this question is to review the original mortgage document. If it is assumable, the document will say so. It may say that it is assumable based on several requirements, and not just "freely assumable." That would essentially mean that any warm body can just take over making the payments on your mortgage. Many banks and other lenders will currently indicate that the mortgage is assumable with a credit check, or a loan-processing fee (equal to a few hundred dollars or perhaps up to several points). They may have several other stipulations, which might include that the new borrower be an owner occupier as well as make the payments in your usual timely fashion. You need to read the document. It spells it all out very plainly.

What if the document states categorically that the mortgage is assumable and the lender says assumable "at the discretion of the lender"? If so, that discretion cannot be unreasonably withheld. I had this situation fall upon me in a transaction I handled back in the mid-'80s. The assumable rate was 7.5 percent and the current rate was 11.75. The rates were going up, and the bank decided to say, based on its own discretion, the mortgage was no longer assumable.

We had to speak to the president of the bank and remind him that this discretion was unreasonable.

Discretion can be based on an inability of the new borrower to demonstrate his ability to repay the loan (questionable credit, for example). That would be the only reasonable determination that would be acceptable. The ability of the bank to lend out new money at substantially higher rates is not a good enough reason. That may not be reasonable from a profit standpoint, but it is tough turkey, as we say.

So how did you do on the quiz? Did you do as well as you thought you would? Did you cheat and just jump ahead to the answers? Were you expecting the answers to be simple responses like yes, yes, no, no? If you were, I think you know by now that the answers to almost all of them could have started with the words, "Yes or no, but that depends on . . . " with a relatively lengthy answer to follow. Real estate is not always black and white.

Chapter 13

Getting the Word Out: Newspapers, the Internet, and More

The medium is the message.
—Marshall Mcluhan

With respect to this chapter, we are now in a jungle. Newspapers make real estate brokers and their agents crazy. As I've mentioned, one of the first things any broker should make clear to his agents and clients is that "Advertising doesn't sell homes; a good agent with a well-priced house is what sells a home." This is, of course, 100 percent correct. Unfortunately, you and I both know that no one is ever going to believe it. This is why, no matter what local newspaper you pick up, you will see tons of very expensive ads showing all sorts of cute and cozy homes in a myriad of price ranges.

Sellers insist that they unequivocally "know" that advertising is going to sell their home. They will browbeat their agent into insisting that the home get advertised all over the place. The agent will blackmail the broker and even threaten to leave and work for a competitor if "his" house isn't advertised enough! And, surprisingly enough, while all of this is going on, everyone knows the premise is pointless in the first place. So if you are going along with my point of view, you must be asking the question, "If this is the case, then why advertise?" Let's take a closer look into the murky world of your classic morning paper. Maybe we will find the answer to this, and maybe we will merely open a Pandora's box of even greater questions to be answered.

Fair Housing Regulations

Warning! Warning! Certain restrictions apply! In this particular case, before we can even discuss the efficacy of advertising we have to look at the dos and don'ts. We're talking Fair Housing Regulations. In 1988 the U.S. Congress passed the Fair Housing Act in order to provide all Americans with an equal opportunity to obtain housing. The act was intended to strengthen the Civil Rights Act of 1968. Part of the Fair Housing Act specifically covers the advertisement of any dwelling for sale or rent. To whom does the act apply? Is it just the Realtor, the professional, the banker? No, my friends out there in Real Estate Land, it pertains to you, too. The Act, quite simply, is all-encompassing and includes everyone.

Being in the business provides some protection because at least there is an awareness of the restrictions. You might say that is little protection. Quite to the contrary, it is a lot when you read the Fair Housing Manual that most real estate offices keep as a handy reference guide. Quoting directly from the manual:

"The people who really need to watch out are:

• Real estate sellers
• Real estate agents
• Landlords
• Property management companies
• Advertising media
• YOU!"

That's a pretty scary warning, don't you think? Wait, it gets better. The manual goes on to state that, "Fines start at $10,000 per violation and civil damages may be awarded to injured parties. Some publishers have been forced out of business because of multi-million dollar settlements in favor of injured parties." After reading that, all I could say was "Wow!" When I recovered, I asked to see the infamous list of restricted words and phrases that could get one into trouble. Now granted some of them are quite obvious and belong on the list. Many should not even be used in polite company. Still others make me scratch my head a little and say, "Come on, guys, give us a break here."

Let's look at some obvious restrictions first. These are some of the things that agents can't say in their ads:

- Indian
- Irish
- Jewish
- Chinese
- Hispanic
- Caucasian
- Latino
- Catholic
- Gays
- Mexican-Americans

Obviously, any ethnic reference is out. Those are clear to anyone, or at least they should be if you have even a bit of common sense. Let's look at some not so obvious inclusions on the "List." Some of these are just plain dopey.

- *Gentleman's farm*—sorry, but this is considered discriminatory against all persons who could possibly be construed as not being gentlemen.
- *Golden-agers only*—that makes a young fella like myself feel awfully left out.

- *Desirable neighborhood*—that's a bad one, I guess, because given the choice some people might want to be in a less desirable neighborhood.
- *Fisherman's retreat*—this is my personal favorite. "What if I don't want to fish? This is America, and if I don't want to fish, you can't make me."

Now those are examples of words and phrases that are absolutely positively out. But much like the Catholic Legion of Decency's list of bad movies, there is a list of questionable terms as well. When you read some of the items on it below, you'll probably say to yourself, "Excuse me, but what's the problem here?"

- Community
- Close to
- Mother-in-law apartment
- Near country club
- Handyman's dream
- Grandma's house
- Near
- Prestigious
- Quiet neighborhood
- Within walking distance of
- Private
- Sophisticated
- Starter home

After reading this list, do you get the feeling that someone has too much time on his or her hands? You be the judge. I am just giving you the rules of the road.

Other restrictions that the Realtor must be leery of involve ads that mislead the public. Examples of this might be where an ad states that the property is in one location that is considered more desirable than another. Persons or companies that are licensed to transact real estate can, in many jurisdictions, be severely censured by their local boards of Realtors or by their appropriate Departments of State. The civilian, oddly enough, is exempt in almost all cases from deliberately misleading the public with respect to advertising. (This is yet another reason to be wary of buying an FSBO house.)

It is important to note that disciplining an agent, or his company, usually occurs only as a result of a specific complaint being made. In most cases, Departments of State have very little manpower to police these sundry infractions. I do, on occasion, get a polite reminder myself that one of my ads (which an agent placed directly without my authorization) is in violation. It will usually be an ad that features something like "St. Martin's parish." This of course is a no-no because it appeals to a specific religious affiliation and, in theory, discriminates against Jewish people, Muslims, etc. Fortunately, I don't get too many reminders with respect to this kind of an ad, and I am able to keep my office out of trouble.

All of this being said, let's get back to the original question: Why advertise? If it in fact doesn't sell the house or the property, what does it do? Here's the answer: It exposes the property to the market and helps build traffic. That's all it does. In point of fact, it is a perversely inefficient use of dollars if that is what it is supposed to do. Really good agents don't advertise their properties all that much. They contact interested parties directly from their individual pools of buyers that they currently have in their spheres of influence. After that, they contact other agents and brokers and have them tap "their" spheres. After that, they go directly to the market and cold-call prospects who might be candidates for the house.

Does Advertising Work?

One of the things I do in my role as sales manager is to counsel agents on how they should or should not spend their money on advertising. Many of them want to take out what I call a vanity ad for a couple of hundred bucks. The ads usually show a picture of them and tell you what a great job they do and how happy their customers are with them. Of course, the intention is that the ads will make you or somebody just like you call them up and have them start working right away on a specific request for either buying or selling a home. Normally, what happens is the agent will tell me that he got a tremendous response the last time he ran an ad like that.

However, after probing the agent, what I usually find to be the case is that his friends and neighbors saw his ad, maybe even another agent told him she saw it, but, *None of these people bought a house from him as a result of the ad!* They all seem to get a warm fuzzy feeling when they see the ad, though. It is kind of like the warm fuzzy feeling a seller gets when he sees his house prominently displayed in the local paper, too. "Yep," he says, "there's my house, by golly." Sometimes he scratches his head and wonders why the picture is so small, or why the ad didn't mention the super heavy-duty nails.

The important thing to remember here is what was the actual impact. Did anyone call or come out as a result? Generally, I will tell my agents that they should take their "couple of hundred bucks" and invest in ten or twenty hours of telemarketing. It makes a lot more sense in terms of return on investment, and it gives you a very accurate picture with respect to effectiveness.

What kinds of ads build traffic? Surprisingly enough, ads that don't really reveal too much. If an agent tells you every-thing about the property in a full-page ad, there is no reason for you to call the agent with any questions. An ad that tells you the price is under $200,000 will get a lot more calls than an ad that tells you the price is $185,000. You see, what the agent is hoping to do is get the chance to talk to you, to find out if the property meets your specific criteria with respect to price, condition, location, and so on. If you get all the information right away in the ad, there is no opportunity to establish a dialogue and, in effect, eliminate that particular property from your search. An ad that mentions a "huge lot" will get more calls than the ad that specifically tells you that the lot is 350 x 400 feet. The very nature of the word "huge" gives the agent the chance to discuss the size of the lot and respond with, "Oh, I see, you really needed something larger." Perhaps they might add, "Oh, I see, that size lot might be a little out of your price range, I have another one that . . ." Please understand, this is not a case of bait-and-switch. Quite to the contrary. It is an effective way of using the power of advertising to draw traffic toward a property so that the sales professional can be given the possibility of building rapport to see if the property "fits" in the first place.

Because of this inherent power of "vagueness" in advertising, many ads will employ puffery that is designed to attract. Many times, however, when the property falls under actual scrutiny, these exaggerated descriptions merely serve to annoy people. One agent I know would put a sign rider stating that "You *must* see inside." When the would-be buyer made an appointment to look at the house, he would discover that it was clearly a dump. The agent would go on to tell him what a great opportunity the house would provide since it could be gotten at a fraction of the price that homes in better condition would sell for in the same area. I find this at the bare minimum "misleading," and personally I would be quite annoyed. It is perfectly legal, though. The agent didn't tell me that the house was in great condition. He merely suggested in the most emphatic terms that, "I should look inside." I inferred that I would be pleasantly surprised. And, because of my misassumption, the agent did get the opportunity to talk to me to find out that I did not want a fixer-upper. I would not work with someone like that, though, simply because I would have thought that I was being had. It's a little too slick for me.

I was really amused when, in a similar vein, I saw an ad state that the property had "room for a basement." What one would quickly realize upon inspecting the premises was that the house had no basement. This is not so much misleading as it is funny, if you think about it.

How much advertising is enough? Can you advertise a property too much? To answer the first question gets to the very point of whether or not advertising (specifically newspaper advertising) is the best and most effective way to build traffic. I would argue in most cases for an unequivocal, possible maybe.

To answer the second question, if you are running your ad week after week, one really has to ask, is there a limit? When is enough too much? Here's the answer: If you have run more than three ads consecutively with no adjustment in price (in the same paper), you run the risk of overexposing the property. Savvy buyers start to think that a particular house has been on the market forever. There must be something wrong with it. This is one of the most common mistakes that "For Sale by Owners" make. Eventually, they tire of no one responding, and they give up and call a broker.

What about display ads versus classified? Well here's my slant on that. Big sexy display ads can really draw in a crowd. If they are:

a. Big and sexy; that is to say, they employ lots of white space and use the talents of good copywriters.
b. Run relatively frequently in versions with alternating copy that is really punchy.
c. Accompanied by a fairly substantial budget, because display advertising is the expensive way to go.

Having said that, classified ads are clearly the preferred approach, both from a cost-effectiveness standpoint as well as from the perspective of reaching your target audience. Think about it for a second. Which is easier for the consumer? Sifting through page after page of display advertising or going to properties that are alphabetically listed by the location and then by price. Those little classified ads in the back of the newspapers may not be very glamorous, but that's where many buyers look first. Why? Quite simply, because it's easier.

Riding the Airwaves

How about radio advertising? Is it effective? Maybe it is. Is it expensive? Definitely! Raising the level of effectiveness depends on two issues. The first issue is frequency; the second is time slot. The best times are arguably what they call "drive time," and, as you might have guessed, those times are also the most expensive. Another plum spot might be at the top or bottom of the hour sandwiching with the news. Even better would be to get either of those spots at the beginning of popular shows like Rush Limbaugh or Howard Stern. Forget the messages or the politics of either of these examples, these guys are incredible draws and that's why those spots cost more. In any event, radio advertising is effective for the people selling the radio spots, but I would seriously question just how well it works to sell houses.

Ditto to the idea of using television as a way to market your home. It is certainly true that most sellers love seeing their house on TV. And I am sure the producers of those shows can quote all sorts of figures and statistics to prove to you just how well their advertising works. But here's the inside scoop. All this talk is an awful lot of sizzle for a fairly puny steak. Real estate agents love to use TV ads not so much to sell houses but to secure listings. They recognize the emotional sway that occurs when they sit down with a prospective seller and tell him, "Oh, and of course I will be advertising your home on our weekly TV show." One good thing about TV advertising is that it can give buyers a quick feel for what the market has to offer. It's kind of like speed-reading the classifieds, only better. However, rarely have I seen someone actually drop the phone and say, "I have to have that house."

A Brave New World

Here's the question that I know you have all been waiting for: What about the Internet?

What is the Internet, anyway? Why is everyone so obsessed with what it does, what they think it can do, and how it will change our lives? Even now, at the beginning of a new century, economists, computer nerds, and real estate brokers alike have only begun to speculate what the impact will be. Its usage has exploded exponentially beyond anything that can even be described, and its possible applications are almost endless.

The National Association of Realtors (NAR) has taken the position that the World Wide Web is the Realtor's friend. In fact, they have developed strategies to ensure that the computer does not replace the real estate agent, which frankly is still a major concern of lots of industry analysts. Many brokers feel that with online mortgages and free access to listing information, the role of the agent in a classical sense will greatly be diminished and perhaps even eliminated eventually. Other industry savants attempt to placate the ever-growing fears of the members with platitudes like "a click of a mouse can't sell a house." Maybe they are right. One thing is for certain and that is that the role of the agent will definitely change, and some great opportunities will be afforded to those shrewd Realtors out there who embrace the role that technology will play in the next decade.

To give you an overview of what has happened already, there are probably thousands (or should I say more accurately hundreds of thousands) of Web sites out there that can provide you with all sorts of information about buying and selling your home, with or without a broker. If you want to go the FSBO route—and lots of luck to you if you do—there are scores of Web sites our there that can get you into the game. The following are my top ten FSBO sites. I am not endorsing any of them, but if you are a hardhead, take a look. My hope is that after you have had your fun, you will get serious and get yourself a good agent. Here are the sites, and remember they are in no particular order:

- FSBOcentral.com
- FSBOfreedom.com
- Buyowner.com
- Abetterfsbo.com
- Ahome4sale.com
- 2BuyHomes.net
- 4salebyowner.com
- ByOwnerSales.com

One caveat: Because agents know just how unsuccessful homeowners are at trying to sell their own houses, really sharp people in the business use these FSBO sites as prospecting tools. But no matter, the NAR has been smart enough to protect its members from the free and uncontrolled dissemination of its listing inventory by creating the all-time best site anywhere. It is called "Realtor.com" and it can be accessed by anyone out there with the ability to surf the net. It is light years ahead of anything else that is available today. To date it has over 1.3 million properties listed, and the inventory it places each day on this super site seems to be without limit. They also report that each of their listings are averaging about ninety views a day.

Here are some other pretty nifty sites. Homegain.com is a site that boasts no direct affiliation with any other real estate company. One of the cooler things you can do here is anonymously compare top performing real estate agents in your area.

Looking for a mortgage? Surf over to mortgageExpo.com. This site can provide you with useful information beyond mortgage rates. If you are concerned about less than perfect credit, or buying a new home versus an existing home, this site might be a good place to start. But with respect to getting a mortgage online, let me really stick my neck out by saying unequivocally, *"Don't do it!"* Online mortgages are the strangest thing I have seen in the real estate business.

On the surface, it would *seem* perfectly logical to say that getting a mortgage online would be quick and easy and less expensive. "What the heck," one might say, "it's only a bunch of numbers that have to get crunched, right?" Certainly, it seems that this would be a service that would really lend (pardon the pun) itself to a successful marriage with the Internet. But you know what, to date every deal that I have seen that attempted to implement financing via the Internet was a fiasco. I am not saying some deals; I am saying *every* deal. Most of my agents who have been involved in a transaction where Internet financing has been provided turn pale when a buyer comes and tells them, "Oh, I'm getting my mortgage on the Internet." In their experience, the loans historically took longer and had all sorts of problems.

Having said that, if you want to go to these kinds of sites for information, great. Also, I am in no way singling out or condemning mortgageExpo.com. My only reason for mentioning it here is that it seems to be a user-friendly, reliable source for information.

Here's something else that I have observed. One of the coolest things about the net, and not just Realtor.com per se, is the quality of the shoppers that use it. In my own offices, customers who call us in reference to a property they saw listed on the Web are almost always great to work with. They're smart. They know what they are looking for, and what's more important; they know where to get the information. They are also savvy, so they probably know a lot more about financing and economics in general. Frankly, they are just intrinsically more qualified to deal in the real estate market than the buyers and sellers of yester-year *sans* computer. One of the local clothing merchants in New York, Sy Simms, has a slogan, "An educated consumer is our best customer." Net customers are "educated," and they are rapidly proving that this is the way to do business right now, not ten years from now.

Buying habits have changed, and the Internet is now not just the number one source for information on properties, it is the first source that consumers use to access the information. Studies by the National Association of Realtors show us that 86 percent of all buyers go to the Web first and then contact a given real estate agent.

Sensing this avalanche of change, NAR has solicited its members to take out Web pages on Realtor.com, and the smart ones are lining up to do so. For a few hundred dollars, each agent can, in essence, open up his own little shop on the net, and, with proper hyperlinking, he can have you looking up his own listings from his personal inventory amidst a sea of other equally available properties. You will gain just enough information from the site so that you can either call the agent or e-mail him or her requesting additional information. That's what the agent wanted from you in the first place. The only difference is that instead of using newspaper advertising, agents can use a much smarter and more fiscally responsible way to target the audience. Incidentally, the number one reason that broker/owners are investing in Internet technology is the possibility of substantially reducing the cost of their print advertising.

There are lots of other real estate sites out there positioning themselves to grab market share in this hot new medium, so take advantage of the offerings and search to your heart's content. Look under "real estate" and watch how your search engines retrieve a multitude of sites. (You might just start with Smartpages.com and see where it takes you.) Many of them are good but none compare to the depth and quality of Realtor.com. After all, NAR is made up of the most authoritative people in the business.

You might also check out IOwn.com. It's a good second source. In addition to property listings, their site includes mortgage services that allow users to search for homes that might be of interest to them. You might also punch a few keys and determine the property value. Heck, you can even find an agent. Ned Hoyt, the CEO of IOwn.com, recently acquired another site known as Homegain, in an effort to grab a larger piece of the real estate info-market. The combination of the two sites is expected to bring in well over a half a million users each month. It will be interesting to see what Realtor.com's response will be. I'll wager there will be lots of added services. The competition is good for them and, ultimately, great for the consuming public. Needless to say, the Internet can be an invaluable tool when looking to buy or sell your home. There is more information readily available to consumers than ever before, so take advantage of it.

Chapter 14

Buying and Selling: Rules to Live By

I just got wonderful news from my real estate agent in Florida. They found land on my property.

—Milton Berle

ow that you have some of the basics under your belt, let's give you thirty-six—that's right, three dozen—hard-and-fast rules to help you make the best deal you can. Some of this might serve as a review, but as good coaches always remind their players during half-time pep talks, "You've got to look at basic skills. So remember the fundamentals."

1. *Surround yourself by experts in their respective fields.* You should build your team with proven professionals. You'll need a savvy real estate attorney and a good accountant and, as you learned in Chapter 9, a good real estate agent. If you are able to tap into the information that they all offer, you can achieve all the goals you set for yourself.

2. *Always use a mortgage banker for financing.* Listen to their recommendations. A good one will not simply take a mortgage application. A good one will ask the right kinds

of questions that will enable them to shop the market for the best mortgage product that is out there today to suit your specific needs. Also, they can always shift your application without charging you each time. You never know if you might have to change lenders in midstream if, for example, some "nicks and dings" appear on your credit.

3. *Never buy unless you want to buy.* I know that sounds silly. But many people get so wrapped up in the emotion of the negotiation that they forget what their goals were in the first place and invariably end up paying more than they should.

4. *Remember what negotiation is all about: offer and counteroffer.* No one should ever be insulted at an offer. This is true regardless of how ridiculous the price may seem. What makes the offer insulting is not the "lowness" of the price so much as the manner or the attitude in which it is conveyed. It is crucial that whoever conveys the offer is a person who can do so in a calm and objective manner. No "prima donnas" need apply here. I have no patience for those agents that deliberately let their emotions and attitudes get in the way of the negotiation. If you're doing the negotiation yourself (which is not the recommended approach), keep your head and remember it is just a negotiation.

5. *Remember that everything is negotiable.* The worst that can happen to you is that somebody says, "No," or at worst, he thinks you're silly or cheap.

6. *Try to never break the five-year rule.* If you are planning to sell your property less than five years after you purchase it, you almost always will get hurt. Even if you make a slight profit, your soft costs most certainly will erode any possible gain. Now if you see the chance to make a killing and are in a highly inflationary economy, then go for it. But if you choose this as a strategy you will not agree with number 7.

7. *Never sell unless you have to sell.* I am an advocate of buying and holding on forever. Buying, selling, and flipping

can make for short-term gains, but it doesn't usually build long-term wealth, or dynasties for that matter.

8. *You should only sell if there are no financial options left to provide for the next move.* Benjamin Franklin is credited to have said that, "If you wanted to ensure economic ruin, one should move five times." If you can keep one house and buy the next one, even with leverage, good and proper financing will bring "the benefit of time" to your cause and will help you build great wealth.

9. *When looking for a broker, remember to review his R.E.C.O.R.D., as described in Chapter 9.* Don't use just anybody you bump into. Don't use your best friend or a relative unless you're damned sure she is phenomenal at her job. Even then, you are better off with a competent stranger, because as we pointed out earlier, you can't fire your best friend or your mother-in-law. Remember the words of Don Corleone: "It's nothing personal, it's business." It will get you out of lots of awful social situations that leave you feeling obligated.

10. *Don't buy a "For Sale By Owner" on your own.* For all of the reasons described in Chapter 5, use a good broker. Your exposure is too great to blaze this trail alone. If you have to go that route, hire a buyer's agent even if you have to pay him yourself. I know I discussed earlier in the book that his compensation is normally built into the sales price, and it is paid out as a convenience of the transaction. That's fine. If you can't get the deal to go that way (and heaven only knows why you can't), pay him out of your own pocket and know that you got a better deal than you would have as a lamb being led to slaughter.

11. *Use the skills of a good home inspector.* When buying, this is not the time to get penny-wise and pound-foolish. A home inspector is an important part of the team recommended in item #1. This person will do two things for you: First, he will help you to decide whether or not you want to proceed with the sale; second, he will call to your

attention any deferred maintenance you might expect over the next five years or so. There is a third thing that a good inspector should do for you—help you sleep like a baby after you move in.

12. *Don't buy the best or the most expensive house on the street.* If you do, you had better make sure that your ego is not so big that it really doesn't bother you when your neighbors call you a "pompous ass" behind your back. But more importantly, having the best house on the street will almost always mean that you will sell for less than you should when the time comes.

13. *Buy the worst house on the best street.* After you tie up the purchase, fix up the house. This does three things: First of all, it spurs the economy and provides employment for the people you hire to do the work. Second, it makes the most sense from an investment standpoint. And thirdly, it makes you a better neighbor and a good citizen. Now I know that may sound corny. However, it still makes the most sense regardless of the reasons that you use to justify the logic.

14. *When working with a mortgage banker (lender), ask which of their "junk fees" they are waiving.* Just asking this one question could save you hundreds of dollars. With all the money you will save by asking this question, you will be able to buy lots of copies of this book and give them to your best friends and all the people you really care about.

15. *Look to work with a broker who can offer you "bundled services."* In the age of one-stop shopping you should be able to find a broker in your area who can offer you multiple services in addition to just helping you buy or sell a house. Offering these added services creates a definite profit stream for the broker, but it also passes substantial savings on to you the consumer. It is a better deal for everyone and it usually moves the transaction along that much more quickly. Why? Because the broker has a bigger stake

in the transaction when he has added sources of revenue from mortgages, etc. It's also so much easier on you, because in theory, you have someone who can quarterback the sale and move you toward closing the deal faster.

16. *Don't be afraid to ask the broker about resale.* Granted, she cannot make actual predictions on a potential home. She can, however, give you a true estimation of what has occurred in the specific market in which you are thinking of making a purchase. She can tell you what happened over the last ten years, five years, two years, or six months. Draw your own conclusions, based on watching or learning what the trend has been.

17. *When making purchases of multiple dwellings, remember this: If you want a single, buy a single.* If you want a double, go ahead and buy a double. Don't buy a single, and try to make it into a double. It is invariably more expensive to add or delete a unit than it is to just find the right property that suits your needs in the first place.

18. *Get it in writing!* Everyone should know this one by now. What most people *don't* know is that oral agreements are binding between principals and brokers. They are just not worth the paper they're printed on, as the saying goes. Rather than sounding jaded here, it is not that you shouldn't trust the other parties. It's that having everything in writing eliminates all possible confusion, and it is a definite cure for that thing called the faulty memory.

19. *Don't be afraid to buy the first property you look at, if it suits your needs.* You may ask to see other properties so your decision is based on some sort of comparison. But if you see a good deal, recognize it and go for it. Don't be one of those truly ridiculous people who wants to hold out for an even better deal. There will always be a better deal out there somewhere. All you should really be looking for is a good deal. Letting good deals slip through your fingers because of an insatiable quest to squeeze out a better deal is like a dog chasing its tail and is about as productive.

20. *Owning is better than renting.* That seems fairly obvious. There are times, however, when renting is appropriate. Renting is a poor short-term solution for an occupancy problem, at best. Sometimes, it is still necessary as part of an overall game plan. Buy as soon as it is economically feasible to do so. Renting for more than two years in any given location is usually fiscally imprudent if not downright irresponsible.

21. *Learn for the sake of learning.* Take classes. Go to seminars. Become the kind of buyer and/or seller who knows what she's talking about. Read books on the subject. There is a great selection of recommended books in the back of this book that can give you a good head start. Above all, if you don't know, ask questions. There truly are no stupid questions when it involves a lot of money, especially when it is your money.

22. *Trust your instincts.* They are almost always right on the mark. If something just doesn't feel right, find out why. It is not just your imagination. Now I am not talking about buyer's or seller's remorse here. If those feelings do creep in, it is nothing to worry about either. Talk to your agent (or yourself for that matter). This is the opportunity that he should have to resell you on the benefits of the particular program at hand. That's part of his job. That's why they call it a "sales" job.

23. *Look for properties with high assumable mortgages.* It is usually cheaper to assume a mortgage than it is to get new financing. You will be building equity faster on someone else's mortgage than you could have on your own.

24. *Owner financing is usually more attractive than bank financing.* You might be required to put more money down, but the rest of the package is so much better. You'll save a bundle on closing costs alone.

25. *If you can afford the slightly higher payment, always go for a fifteen-year mortgage, as opposed to the conventional thirty.* The payment is not that much higher and

you'll build equity so much faster. You will also save literally tens of thousands of dollars on interest over the life of the loan. Do the math. You will be absolutely astounded at the savings.

Just to give you an idea, let's look at a $100,000 property note. The total payments when financed at 8 percent over thirty years add up to $264,160. The same amount over fifteen years is $172,018. What's the difference? $92,142 in interest alone, that's what. The difference in the payment each month is only $222. A $734 payment versus a $956 payment. Is a payment that is a couple of hundred dollars higher (for fifteen fewer years) worth it? You be the judge.

26. *By law, all commissions are negotiable.* In some cases, the broker says 7 percent and you say 6 percent and he simply says, "No." That's called negotiating. But you know what, a lot of times the broker will say, "Yes." I am embarrassed to admit this, but my profession is the biggest collection of pussycats you could ever imagine. We have to take special training to learn how to say no. Yes, I am serious. There are tapes and seminars offered that instruct us on "How to Protect Our Commission." In the majority of cases, if you ask to get a break on the commission, you will. Try asking your doctor to reduce his fee. What part of "No" don't you understand? Ask a broker, and seven times out of ten, he will roll right over for you. Try it. If you save a point just for being stubborn you deserve it, and that can mean a lot of money in your pocket. One thing is for certain, there are almost no brokers out there (or very few) who won't buckle at the eleventh hour. It is truly something for which we should be ashamed of as an industry.

The closer the broker gets to closing, the more likely he is to cave. This, my friends, is truly one of the biggest insider secrets this book offers to you, the bold consumer. So, dig in your heels, and go for the jugular. In my opinion, the broker should tell you to pound salt. He has already earned his commission. He'll probably yield, though. My colleagues will probably want to have me tarred and feathered for telling you this one.

27. *If you're selling, here's a case where you can really save big.* Should you find yourself in the following scenario, read this part very closely. On some not so rare occasions, an agent will approach a seller who either does not have his house on the market or is trying to sell it on his own. The agent will ask if he can show the house to a prospective buyer he is working with, and if the seller would be willing to "cooperate with them." The seller obliges the agent without seeing any harm in the matter. Very soon afterwards the agent will come back with a signed offer on the house from that same customer. Great for the seller, you say. The agent at that point will try to negotiate a commission into the transaction. This is kind of like having someone paint your house and then ask you to pay him after the fact. What is the alternative at that point, taking the paint off the house? We've already said that commissions are negotiable, but that is not the problem in the example we have described here.

The issue is that the commission was never negotiated up front. How can an agent just tack on a commission after the fact and expect to get paid? It beats me. Agents must always disclose whom they are working for and what their fee is. If the agent had asked what the price of the house was and said, "Fine, my fee is X percent of the sale price," that would have been swell. That's not what happened here. As silly as this sounds, this kind of thing goes on every day, much to the embarrassment of brokers everywhere. So how is this going to save money for anyone? The simple fact of the matter is that the seller owes the agent nothing. That's right—nada, zip, nothing. The agent can scream all he wants to at that point, but, frankly, he is the one who screwed up. Because there was a failure to disclose, there is no fee due. If an agent messes up in this manner, I feel very strongly that he should get exactly what is due him: nothing.

28. *Never pay the asking price.* Even the seller knows that isn't the real price you should pay. When I wrote the first draft of this book, one of my colleagues read this and said, "You don't really mean this, do you?" She went on to question my usage of the word *never.* She further carped that buyers "pay the asking price all the time and frequently pay over the asking price, especially in competitive offers." That's absolutely true. My colleague actually should have questioned the usage of the term *asking.* When I say one should never pay the asking price, I am telling you to ask yourself if that is the real price. Are the sellers boldly asserting that the price is such and such, and that's it? Or are they really cautiously "exploring" (with you as the market maker) what you really think it is worth? If instead of *telling* you the price, they are only sheepishly *asking,* you should *ask* if they'll accept something less and pay them accordingly.

Here's something else related to price. No matter how much you love a house, determine the value based on price per square foot. You can decide to pay whatever you deem is acceptable. You can pay the market price. But remember this, even though all houses have a bankable uniqueness to them, you might not want to get stuck paying significantly more on a square foot basis than comparable houses in the area. Maybe it won't matter if you can afford to take a hit at resale time. If it (the value per square foot/ratio) does come into play, however, and there is a noteworthy discrepancy, ask the agent what's the story. Depending on the answer, you may choose to lower the offering price, stay put because of the property's uniqueness, or pass on the property altogether.

29. *Location, location, location.* This one is so obvious I tried to slip it in where it was least expected. There is no substitute for a good location.

30. *Sometimes great terms can offset a lousy location.* As I've mentioned, I will buy any piece of property at any price, *if* I can name the terms. (How about a dollar down

and a dollar a week . . . forever.) You would be surprised how many sellers will consider insane terms just to get rid of a property. I recently witnessed a big commercial building in downtown Buffalo get sold at what is known as a reverse auction. Because no one was willing to pay for the relatively elegant building in the heart of the commercial district, the seller paid someone to take it off his or her hands. That's right, the seller paid someone well over a half a million dollars to take it off his hands. It was a good deal for both parties since it was costing the seller a million and a half to carry it each year. If you want to be a smart buyer, then always look for a motivated seller.

31. *Take out a thirty-year mortgage and make one extra principal payment each year.* That will save you about eight years on the mortgage and a boatload of interest payments.

32. *When you are selling a house, your first offer is probably your best offer.* Holding out for a higher offer will almost always result in disappointment down the road.

33. *Sometimes, a good tenant paying under the market is worth his weight in gold.* Some property managers will tell you to constantly raise your rents. This can result in unnecessary vacancies and properties that are difficult to manage. Don't get too greedy. Sometimes stability is just as important as higher rent payments.

If you have to raise rents, do it very gradually. Doing it in this manner lets the tenant know that rents go up the same way that a loaf of bread increases year after year. There will be no shock, and you won't have a panicked and resentful tenant on your hands.

34. *Two things will tell you if a property is well maintained: the basement and the roof.* Everything else really kind of falls into place if those two places are in good order.

35. *If you want to buy a house, don't ask your parents what they think unless they are real estate brokers or are in the business somehow.* Their opinions may be of interest, but have little merit. They will also make you nuts and

probably keep you from making a good deal that is fairly based on *today's* market. This is, as opposed to the market of twenty or thirty years ago when they bought their first house.

36. *Lastly, remember the time value of money.* If you are selling, know how long it should take to sell your home and price it accordingly. In the business, it is known as the "turnover rate." Taking an extra six months will cost you big-time, not just in carrying costs but in actual dollars lost from the price the property would have sold at if it were priced realistically from the get-go. If you are buying, you should set a timetable for yourself as well. Do not hold out for that perfect "pie in the sky" deal. If you do, it will keep you from getting a really good deal that would be perfectly adequate for most people.

Chapter 15

When You're in Trouble, Whom Should You Call?

I know the answer! The answer lies within the heart of all mankind! The answer is twelve? I think I'm in the wrong building.

—Charles Schulz

Yikes! Things aren't going the way you thought they were supposed to go. Now what do you do? Well, you could do what most people would do. First, you start to talk to all your friends and acquaintances who will be more than willing to stick their noses into your business. They are vastly ill-equipped to give you any sort of advice in most cases. Some may feel obligated to "help" you. Fine! Say thank you and resist heeding their warnings at all costs, unless you want to really make your life miserable.

In most cases, when a real estate transaction starts to go bad, it is little less than a simple misunderstanding between either the principals or the agents, or both. Assume that there is nothing to panic about and start at the first line of offense. It is really crucial to remember the chain of command in a transaction. Following the proper chain will spare you great embarrassment at the bare minimum and great expense if taken to the ultimate extreme. To put this in perspective, at the first sign of a wrinkle in the transaction, it would be silly to try to bring a class action suit. Wouldn't it? It would be as ludicrous as hunting for rabbits with a nuclear bomb. You might end up killing an awful lot of rabbits, but what a mess you have created, and there is probably no way to recover what you wanted in the first place.

Always start with the agent. If you don't understand why things are not going the way you "assumed," ask the agent to explain why. In 90 percent of the cases you are probably wrong and everything is going according to plan, or at least as the Contract of Sale has indicated is the correct way to proceed. Don't go to your lawyer right away. If you do, he'll either make it worse or just start charging you more money. If the answer seems less than satisfactory, move the bar up one notch only. Ask to speak to the manager. Now you are at Step Two.

When you ask to speak to the manager, the smart thing to do is to ask the agent if he or she wouldn't mind if you could discuss the matter with the manager. This does two things. It gives the agent a last chance to either address your concerns to your liking or fix it (if it has become broken), and it does something else, too. It gives the agent a chance to review the matter with the manager before you start to rant and rave. This will further provide the manager with an opportunity to review the file and have a working familiarity with the transaction before you stampede into his office and make a spectacle of yourself. No matter what you tell the manager at that point, the response will normally be, "Let me take a look at the file."

Managers do this so they can put together in their own minds exactly what they need to say or what they need to do to effectively intervene. Most managers are swamped with work and need a few moments to review the specifics of your deal and sort it out from the hundreds of others they are juggling at any given time.

Asking the agent's permission will also allow the agent to save face. It will further provide the agent with the opportunity to present your side of the story, and his own, to the manager in the most favorable light. If you just call the manager directly, she won't know what you're talking about initially, and she will ask you to either "hold" while she checks the file or "hold" while she reviews the matter with the agent and "gets back to you." Presenting your argument this way invariably puts everyone on the defensive and gets less favorable results, albeit sometimes a more timely response.

If that doesn't work, now it's time to call the lawyer, right? Well, this is where I would say, "Not exactly." If the manager isn't able to give you the kind of answers you think you should be getting, ask to speak to the next person up the ladder. Step Three should lead to either the general manager or the broker in charge, or the president of the company. Depending on the size of the firm, this could be the same person, or it could be several different people. I would advocate that you stick to the chain of command for a number of reasons. Going right to the top is kind of sneaky and undermines the people below. Most importantly, it doesn't win you any points. At some time in the not so distant future, you will probably be seeing people like the manager and/or the agent in the community in which you are doing your business. They will remember how you treated them. You may close the deal, but you will also have to live in the community. You don't want to hear things such as, "You know that so-and-so is a real pain in the you-know-what." No matter how you cut it, it is almost always bad form to end-run anyone or everyone. There is a time for that. It is just not the time, not just yet.

Step Three is usually as far as you need to go. The general manager's job is to make sure nothing gets to the big boss. He acts like the goalie in a championship hockey match. He looks really bad if you slip one past him. He wants to get it fixed like nobody else does. He will most likely be your strongest support. You will get the best advice at this level. It should invariably be the smartest and least time-consuming route to follow, and more than likely, the most cost effective. General managers need everything to go away quickly and painlessly to keep their positions. It's true that owners of companies will want to help you, but if it has gotten to their level they can turn on you and say, "Go ahead and sue us. Make my day." Try to stay at Step Three. If this doesn't work, it is time for Step Four. Gulp.

Now you have arrived (even if only by phone) at the sanctum sanctorum. You are dealing with the great Oz himself, the president. If you are actually sitting in the office, he or she will be the epitome of grace and good manners. He will be the hallmark of compassion, as he attempts to build rapport with you and asks how "he might help you?" He will be sincere in asking, because he doesn't need the aggravation either. After listening patiently, he will usually bark out some orders to his assistant and give the impression (sometimes the illusion) that he is really going to take matters into his own hands and resolve the issue immediately. If he doesn't, it is usually bad news and you are going to reach an impasse where no one from the company will be able or willing to resolve you problem. It is time for Step Five. Oh, boy, fasten your seat belts.

"Get Me My Lawyer!"

Now you can call your attorney. You have given the so-called good guys a fair shot at dealing with the issue at hand. Now it's time to talk to Mr. Nasty. Initially, your attorney will want to take a very hard-line approach. You should ask your lawyer if you should deal with the other principal in the transaction directly. Many times "the one man to another approach" is all you to have to do to get things back on track. Having one lawyer talk to the other lawyer is fraught with a myriad of expensive and painful possibilities. What "going to the attorney" does for you at this point is to give you a clearer understanding as to the seriousness of the situation and the best way for you to act. But be careful. Allowing the attorney to act here merely guarantees an adversarial position from this point forward with virtually everybody but specifically with the principals. That may be your best option, of course, but weigh the pros and cons before you get too far into the legal maze.

When you get to Step Five, you need to be especially cautious. Ironically, you will need to rid yourself of the notion of what's "moral" or "right or wrong." This is presuming, of course, that you have a greater concern for your financial well-being. What becomes crucial when attorneys are involved is your clear understanding of the concept known as "downside risk." You need to know, if you take this particular approach, what exactly is the full potential of your total loss; to put it in another way, how much will it cost you in the worst-case scenario.

An overly strident position will cost you big-time in virtually all cases. I see this all the time in situations where I've asked sellers or purchasers to look at the big picture. I ask them, "Do you want to lose a deal and get sued by arguing over a stove?" The depreciated cost may only be $125. The one party making the claim may be legally and morally entitled to it. But, come on now, if it is only worth $125, is it worth going to the mat and letting the attorneys charge ten to a hundred times as much to resolve it? Cut the deal! Let go of your need to be right and get on with life.

Let me fast-forward the situation a bit. Perhaps you reasoned that discretion was the better part of valor and you have closed on the property. You're still looking for satisfaction from somebody. There are several routes available to you depending on the nature of the perceived infraction. If your beef is with the agent or the company that was working with you, you have some choices.

Whom Else Can You Call?

Remember I said earlier that all agents were "licensed"? As such, their actions let them fall under the scrutiny of the particular jurisdiction of the Departments of State in which they are practicing. You can immediately lodge a formal complaint with the Department of State, or, those of us in the business call it, the "DOS." This does a couple of things. It puts the broker on notice. There will be a specific investigation, and frankly it is such a pain in the butt that merely hinting that you are considering doing this usually will get you what you want.

The Department of State has very broad powers with respect to policing those whom they license. Regardless of the outcome, the broker doesn't want to have it on his record that he has been cited. Truth be told, there are so many frivolous complaints that it really makes the system unfair for brokers. That's why they will snap to attention if they think they are going to have to deal with your complaint one step higher, rather than dealing directly with you, which would have been so much easier. By the way, it is a pain in the butt for you, too. You will have to file it in writing, and make your complaint sound somewhat substantive. In addition, it is best to send your complaint certified or registered mail to the Department of State. All of their correspondences with the broker, after they receive your complaint, will be certified mail, up until the actual hearing where everybody will be present in person.

If you are working with an agent who is also a Realtor, you can take another route by complaining to the local board or association to which the Realtor belongs. You can cite him or her for grievances, ethics, or monetary damages. Brokers and their agents will be almost as perturbed by being summoned before the local association as they will be by the DOS. The association has significant clout, too. They can severely censure their members and inflict fines and penalties. In the most severe cases, they can eject them from the association. The DOS can actually put them out of business, though, and that makes for a much stiffer penalty.

When I set out to write this chapter, I thought I would mention the various names and addresses of the different associations you could complain to, but I was unaware of just how many there are. I thought, well let's see, if there are fifty states, there might be two or three associations per state. It would be a long list, but a manageable one. You could look up just the right person and make your complaint if you were so inclined.

Amazingly enough, there are well over 1,700 different local boards and associations affiliated with the National Association of Realtors. I should have realized this, of course. After all, we are talking about the largest trade organization in the world with more than 800,000 members. So needless to say, I am not including the list. If you want to know whom to contact at your local association, you can look it up in the phone book. That's what I did. In fact, I called my local association in Buffalo, which happens to be one of the largest in the country, and they were very helpful. If you want the whole list of associations, you can go to the Internet and look it up on *www.realtor.com*. You'll find whatever and whomever you need to make your initial inquires and complaints right there. You can also visit *www.realtor.org*.

What about just going to small claims court? That may be an option, too. Sellers can take buyers there. Buyers can take sellers there. It is an inexpensive and efficient route. It is the "People's Court" method of establishing quick justice. One major downside is that you are limited to a certain monetary amount that may not cover your entire claim. In my local jurisdiction, we are limited to claims not exceeding $5,000. Principals can sue brokers there as well.

Unfortunately, the system can become unfair and even perverse against brokers, because many shady buyers and sellers look to force brokers to settle for relatively small amounts rather than going to small claims court. Most brokerages are "incorporated," and most small claims courts will not let corporations defend themselves without an attorney. In those cases, litigants reason that it is probably cheaper for the broker to concede to a smaller amount (one might call this legalized extortion) than to incur legal expenses with expensive attorneys. Smaller brokers will often yield to unreasonable demands and figure it is just cheaper to cut a deal than it is to go to court. Larger companies will usually stand on principle and "go to court." They have more to lose in the long run, if the word gets out that they are willing to roll over to these kinds of pressure tactics. Because of this, they really can't afford to forego their principles. Thank goodness for that.

Whatever route you explore as you look to get the results that you expected, remember to make inquires from persons or groups that are empowered to respond. By that I mean, and I cannot stress this strongly enough, don't ask your friends. Unless they are "interested" parties in the specific transaction, keep away from their best free advice. Talk to your agent, or to his manager. Talk to the broker in charge or talk to the other principal. Talk to the attorneys, talk to the escrow agent, talk to the insurance carrier, talk to the loan rep. Heck, you can even talk to the underwriter if you have to, but leave your friend's advice alone if you want to save yourself a bundle and maintain your friendships. Now if you have been brave enough to act without an agent, just skip the part about talking to your agent. Talk to anyone else on the list. Follow the steps I've outlined in this chapter. Likewise, leave your friends out of it. Regrettably, you will only appreciate this advice if you don't take it, and you bring the pain and suffering onto your friends. Then you will have wished that you heeded the warning.

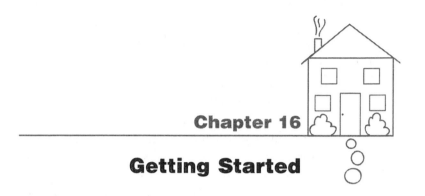

Chapter 16

Getting Started

Don't let it end like this. Tell them I said something.
　　　—Last words of Pancho Villa (1877–1923)

e are living in changing times, and the strategies
that can help each of us realize the American
Dream of owning our ideal home are changing
faster than ever. If we are to better equip ourselves to deal
in the very specialized financial arena of real estate, we
must understand the role of the real estate broker and the
agents. By now you must realize that, by and large, I see
these agents as the good guys. In essence, this book is
designed to give you a step-by-step approach to buying
and selling real estate so that you can understand how to
use the broker to more efficiently realize your goals. So
what do you do now?

The first thing you should do is "decide." Decide what
it is that you want to accomplish. With a clear decision in
mind you should set out to formulate a business plan that
makes the most sense for your current and future needs. At
a minimum, it should be a five-year plan. You should gath-
er as much information as possible and begin to pick your

team as we described in the previous chapter. Once you have selected your team of professionals, it comes time to pick the most important person in the process. You must pick your real estate broker. If you don't remember the process we used, check back and review this particular section in Chapter 9. Where to begin? If you don't get an exceptionally strong endorsement from one of your closest advisors, immediately use the "interviewing the manager approach" to secure the right person for the right job.

You surely realize by now, that the agent you choose to work with is the key to your success. Your agent acts as a fiduciary, a relationship that implies "great trust." Make sure this very special person is one that deserves your trust and demonstrates unimpeachable competence in his field.

You have already learned that to take up the search to buy or sell alone without a broker's assistance is pretty foolish in both the short and long run. If you are still not convinced of that then you should reread Chapter 5. If you can get an experienced guide to lead you through the wilderness and you could build it into the price you were going to pay when you set out, why wouldn't you want it? If you are pigheaded that's one thing, but get over it. If you are one of these people who claims they have had a bad experience with a broker, so what? Go and find a broker who makes sense. If you are such a "know-it-all" that you, absolutely, positively, think you know everything there is to know about the market, I feel sorry for you. If you think "all" agents are jerks, run and get your money back on this book. Granted, some agents are pretty dopey. But if that's what you are convinced of, you should be writing a book of your own. I am certainly not claiming to know everything, but my twenty-plus years of selling and sales-manging experience in real estate has taught me more than a few things.

So go get yourself an agent and begin assembling your team. Leave your sense of self-righteousness at the door, because that will always cost you more than it is worth. And remember to ask questions politely. People are much more willing to help you get what you want when you show some courtesy and *savoir-faire*. If everyone, from the broker to the home inspector, is relaxed with the process, then everyone will get his or her mutual goals met much more easily. If you think everyone is out to screw you, then they will probably end up doing that. Conversely, if you think everyone is a lady and/or a gentleman and is looking out for your interest, you are being naïve. Remember, that's why you should be using a good agent. Of course, it won't hurt to have a good attorney in the wings, either. But before you start getting nervous and begin thinking about all the whys and wherefores and what can go wrong, please keep one last thought in mind.

Buying, selling, or investing in real estate is one of the biggest parts of realizing the American Dream, and rightfully so. It is no accident that we are the number-one nation in the world when it comes to home ownership. No other country boasts as high a rate of home ownership as the good old U. S. of A. Right now it is at an all-time high at nearly 68 percent. There is nothing to indicate that the rate will go down soon, either. In fact, there is no reason to think that it will do anything but go up. This is especially true considering interest rates are at a thirty-year low, and banks are practically begging people to come in and borrow money to buy a house. Virtually every state in the union is also offering some kind of a low-down-payment program for first-time buyers. So if you aren't in the game, what are you waiting for?

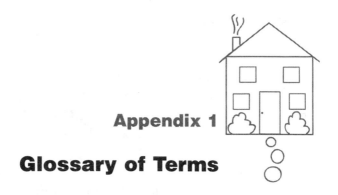

Appendix 1

Glossary of Terms

adjustable rate mortgage (ARM):
The interest on these loans and/or mortgages is periodically adjusted up or down, usually depending on a specified financial index. Classic business strategy assumes that a fixed rate is better than an adjustable rate. This is not always the case, especially when fixed rates are high. One can always take a lower adjustable rate in the hopes that long-term fixed rates will drop low enough to make sense for the borrower to refinance. Make sure that the adjustable rate that you get is not so low that it doesn't keep pace with the index, resulting in "negative amortization." Always ask the lender if the mortgage carries the possibility of negative amortization. If it does, in the long run it could cost you dearly. Often an ARM is the right choice to make if you know you will only be in the home for a short period of time.

agent:
One who acts on behalf of another, representing that person's interest, and usually acting as an intermediary. An agent in a real estate transaction should serve as a fiduciary and can act of behalf of the buyer, the seller, or both. The agent can even represent another broker. The key question to have resolved in every transaction is, "Whose agent are you?" If you don't know the answer before you ask the

question, you should look for signs of red flags scattered across the field.

annual percentage rate (APR):
The actual finance charge for the loan. Not the teaser rate, this is what you are really being skinned for. This rate includes points and loan fees in addition to the stated loan rate.

appraisal:
An opinion of the value or worth of a property given by a person who hires himself out to be an expert in determining this. An appraisal can be given by a person who has been certified to do appraisals or by licensed real estate agents who are competent in this field. The determination of value is subjective and can be arrived at by a comparative market approach, the cost approach, or combinations of the two. If you don't like one appraisal you can always get another and another. It is not unusual for courts to ask for two or three to determine a "mean" estimate of value.

assessed value:
The value placed on a given property by a municipality for purposes of taxation. It frequently differs widely from appraised or market values. Many brokers feel that these values are randomly determined by assessors, because they sometimes bear no resemblance to anything close to any other value arrived at by normal people.

assignment:
The transfer of rights, liabilities, and obligations to another party without the original party remaining "on the hook." This is similar to an assumption.

assumption (of a mortgage):
A buyer assumes liability for an existing mortgage or note held by a seller. All of this is subject to the approval

of the original lender. Often the original seller is not totally released from the liability in the event that the buyer defaults. If the seller wants this added protection, he or she should request an assignment with a release of liability. This usually comes with an added cost that can be born by the new borrower if it is negotiated into the transaction. This is another example of "Never assume anything."

balloon payment:

A large principal payment that is due all at once at the end of a specific loan term. It is as if the balloon goes "pop" and all hell breaks loose. Sometimes the borrower can ask for an extension if the moneys are not available to pay the mortgagee. If the borrower cannot refinance, we may have the scenario familiar from silent films where the evil landlord is threatening the widow with foreclosure.

binder:

Also known as *earnest money*. A small, but serious, amount of money accompanying an offer to purchase real estate, along with a brief written agreement specifying the salient terms of a sales contract to follow. This is also sometimes referred to as "good faith" money.

broker:

A real estate professional who has attained a higher level of training than an agent. An agent works for a broker. Generally, this is the "man in charge" or the proprietor of the real estate business.

cap:

This is as opposed to the ceiling. The limit on how much the interest rate can change in an ARM during an adjustment period. The ceiling is the total limit the loan can be adjusted over the economic life of the loan. An ARM will therefore have a ceiling and a cap.

certificate of title:
Document signed by a title examiner, stating that a seller has an insurable title to the property.

chattel:
Personal property and all the other stuff that is not real estate. One can have a chattel mortgage as well.

closing:
Also known as "closing the deal," this is the meeting where the deed to the property is legally transferred from the seller to the buyer. Closing also refers to the act in the selling process whereby the salesperson attempts to gain some form of commitment from the party he or she is working with in the transaction. Various closing techniques might be used to gain this commitment including the "Trial" close, the "Assumptive" close, and everyone's favorite, the "Benjamin Franklin" close.

collateral:
Any security on a loan secured through a lender. You have heard of the expression, "Put up, or shut up!" This is what you have to put up if you want to get the money from the person who is giving it.

commission:
A fee (usually set as a percentage of the total transaction) paid to the agent of broker for services performed. Most agents work on commission and do not get a salary. As such, they are only paid if they bring the transaction together. In virtually all cases, if they show you a million houses and do not put the deal together and get that all-important "meeting of the minds," they earn nothing.

comparative market analysis (CMA):
A survey of attributes and selling prices of "comparable"

houses (also called "comps") on the market or recently sold; it is used to help determine the correct pricing strategy for a seller's property. Really good agents think of the CMA as a *competitive* market analysis as opposed to a comparative one. To make the subject property more competitive, the agent will focus on the prices of the competing properties still on the market. The agent will attempt to price the subject at a price slightly lower than the rest of the market. Based on the simple law of "supply and demand," the subject property should therefore appear more attractive in the marketplace and sell more quickly.

condominium:
Usually referred to as simply *condo*, a form of real estate ownership where the owner has title to a specific unit and shares interest in common areas. This type of ownership in common goes back to Roman times, as the Latin origins of the word would indicate.

contingency:
A condition in the contract that must be met for the contract to continue until other terms are met or until the deed actually transfers. The term "subject to" can be substituted. There can be major and minor contingencies in a contract. They can include being contingent on a home inspection, mortgage approval, the sale of other property, attorney approval, etc. If they are unavoidable, contingencies should at least always be limited to a specific time frame.

contract:
Binding legal agreement between two or more willing parties that delineates the conditions for the exchange of value (a.k.a. valuable consideration: money exchanged for title to a property). In most states the "Statute of Frauds" requires that contracts be in writing. See Chapter 1 for a more expanded explanation.

conversion clause:
A provision that allows one to convert an ARM to a more favorable fixed rate after a specified interval.

cooperative (co-op):
A relatively uncommon form of ownership (except for in New York and other larger cities). In a co-op, a corporation is set up and each individual shareholder is granted a proprietary lease for a specific living unit based on the apportioned number of stocks owned.

deed:
The legal document that formally conveys ownership of property from seller to buyer. It is always wise to have deeds recorded at the local county clerk's office to further protect one's rights.

down payment:
Percentage of the total purchase price that the buyer is required to pay in "cash" and may not borrow from the lender. Different kinds of lending options will require more or less depending on the program. VA financing will allow veterans with benefits to get by with nothing down. Conventional financing may require as much as 20 percent or more. It is always best to consult with your mortgage banker to determine which is the best and most beneficial route for you to determine your financing and your down payment options.

earnest money:
In some locations this is the same as the "binder." In others it is a large deposit paid when the sale contract is signed before the closing. The greater the earnest money, the more credible is the offer. Some purchasers may balk when a hefty earnest money deposit is encouraged. However, as in Las Vegas, if you want to get into the game

you have to put money on the table. The higher the stakes, the more money you are expected to bring with you.

escrow:
An actual fund or account held by a third-party custodian known as the "escrow agent" (a fiduciary) until the conditions of the contract are met. Ostensibly, any responsible party can hold an escrow if all parties to the contract agree.

equity:
The value of the property actually owned by the homeowner. The formula for determining this is:

$$\text{Purchase Price} + \text{Appreciation} + \text{Improvements}$$
$$- \text{Mortgages and Liens}$$
$$= \text{Equity}$$

Another way to look at it is to figure it is what you will clear after the deal is done (less taxes and smaller miscellaneous expenses).

equity erosion:
The loss of equity either through depreciation or because of actual damage to the property. When equity erosion occurs, you invariably sell for less than what you paid or less than you have totally invested.

Federal National Mortgage Association ("Fannie Mae," FNMA):
A privately owned corporation created by Congress that buys mortgage notes from local lenders and is responsible for creating the guidelines that a majority of lenders use to qualify their borrowers. Many people in the business think that these are actually government loans, but they are not.

fee simple, fee absolute:
Interchangeable terms to indicate complete ownership of real estate as opposed to leaseholds, tenancies, life estates, freeholds, etc.

fiduciary:
A relationship that establishes great trust where one party acts for another. A fiduciary's obligations include: obedience, loyalty, due diligence, confidentiality, accountability, and reasonable care.

finance charge:
The total cost including all fees, points, and interest payments a borrower pays to obtain credit.

fixed rate mortgage:
This is clearly the backbone of the mortgage business, and it is what everyone would want in a perfect world. Interest rates on this type of a loan remain the same (fixed) over the life of the loan term. It is the opposite of an adjustable rate mortgage (ARM).

fixer-upper:
The golden opportunity where one finds the perfect house that can be fixed up and made better, either for quick resale or to provide a great home through the combined forces of capital and sweat equity.

fixture:
A recognized entity (such as a toilet bowl or a kitchen cabinet or a light fixture) that is permanently attached to the property and belongs to the property when it is sold. The key word here is "attached." If the entity is removed, does it leave a gap or a hole? If it does, it is a fixture and it stays with the property unless otherwise specified in the Contract of Sale.

graduated payment mortgage:
The feature of this mortgage product is that monthly payments start low and increase at a predetermined rate. It differs slightly from the ARM where the actual rate changes, as opposed to the payment itself.

hazard insurance:
This kind of homeowner's insurance compensates for property damage arising from specified hazards such as fire and wind (not floods, which are covered under flood insurance). More complete coverage is issued under all-risk homeowners' insurance.

home inspection report:
A report prepared by a "qualified" inspector (see Chapter 10). It should evaluate in a clear and concise manner the property's structure and mechanical systems. If the parties are dealing in good faith, it should not be used as an opportunity to renegotiate the deal. This is done all the time, but it is the acme of bad form.

interest:
The cost of borrowing money usually expressed as a percentage over time. It is another one of the costs of doing business in the wonderful world of real estate.

key dates:
The dates in a contract that trigger certain events to follow. These dates include: closing dates; mortgage commitment dates; acceptance or deletion of a contingency; approval by a third party such as an attorney, home inspector, spouse, accountant, health inspector, etc.

letter of commitment:
The document that states that a lender will "commit" or agree to actually lend one money under very specific terms.

lien:
A security claim on property until a debt is satisfied. Liens are frequently ranked in order of subordination from first to second, and so on.

listing contract:
Also known as *listing agreement* (it sounds less threatening). It is an agreement whereby an owner engages a real estate agent for a specified period to sell property, for which sale the agent receives a set commission.

market age:
"How long has the property been on the market?" This is a question sure to come up with every buyer. How long a property has been on the market ultimately will affect the final price offered. Obviously, if the property has been on the market for any length of time it should have sold, unless the market was resistant to the price. The greater the market age, the further one can expect to get from the original sales price.

market price:
The actual price at which a property is sold. I like to call it the "strike price."

market value:
The price that is established by present economic conditions, location, and general trends. "Supply and demand" is the immutable indicator of market value.

meeting of the minds:
The buyer agrees to buy and the seller agrees to sell at specific terms and price. In most states the property doesn't actually have to close for the agent to be have earned his commission. They earn it upon the "meeting of the minds" of the two principals.

mortgage:
Security claim by a lender against a property until the debt is paid. Word stems from the Old French "dead glove."

multiple listing service (MLS):
A system that provides its members detailed information about properties for sale. The service also grants to its cooperating members a unilateral agreement of subagency with a standard set of bylaws, which are designed to regulate its usage.

National Association of Realtors (NAR):
Voluntary membership organization with well over a million active participants. Not all agents belong. Membership requires strict adherence to a code of ethics well above what any local laws may require. Members are subject to disciplinary action by the association. The group has the largest political action committee in the country.

negative amortization:
The dreaded "N" word. When this exists, the monthly payments aren't enough to cover interest costs; they are added to the principal balance, and you may end up owing more than when you started. This is most likely to occur with certain kinds of ARMs that have payment caps or with graduated payment mortgages (these are highly unusual). With any mortgage, other than a fixed rate, you should always ask if there is a possibility of negative amortization. It is atypical at present, but it was a standard bill of fare back in the '80s.

origination fee:
The application fee for processing a proposed mortgage. It is frequently equal to "one point." Always ask how much this fee is.

philosophical differences:
"We just don't get along. We don't like the way the other party does business." This is a key reason why many agree to part company and choose to take their business elsewhere.

PITI:
Pronounced pit–ē, it stands for *Principal, Interest, Taxes, and Insurance*. It forms the basis for monthly mortgage payments and is usually lumped together by banks and other financial institutions. They set up escrow accounts to provide for the payments to the insurance companies and/or the local tax authority. Depending on the down payment, certain lenders will wave the escrow and let the borrower make direct payments for taxes and insurance. One should always ask if the monthly payment being quoted includes taxes and insurance. Most agents will quote you the lower rate of principal and interest only. By doing so you seem to be able to afford more house. It can come as a very rude surprise if all of a sudden you receive a tax bill in the mail that you thought was being "escrowed" for you.

point:
One percent of the total amount of the loan. It is charged in addition to interest and fees. Many parts of the country quote interest rates with a certain number of points tacked on. Make sure you ask if the rate includes any points and how many. Ask if the points include the "origination fee" or if it is separate. Don't be shy about asking. It will show that you are nobody's fool and that you take nothing for granted.

possession:
When one party actually takes up residence in a property or relinquishes the same. The title can, but may not actually, pass from one to another. Possession is one of the

five P's and as such it is an essential in a real estate contract. It can be, but it is not necessarily, the same as closing.

prepayment penalty:
A clause that states, to put it plainly, that if you pay the loan off before the entire loan has run its course, it will cost you extra. Prepayment penalties are relatively rare nowadays. Ask the loan officer if the loan you are considering has a prepayment penalty.

prequalification:
Not to be confused with preapproval. This is an informed estimate of how much financing a potential borrower might expect to obtain. The loan officer will usually do this (an agent can do it as well) before the borrower has incurred any substantive loan (fees, got applications, etc.) A preapproval takes the process one step further. After being prequalified the applicant has a full credit check and is actually "approved" for a mortgage up to a specific amount pending an appraisal of the property to be purchased.

principal:
This can refer to one of two things. In the first case, it can refer to the individuals or parties to a real estate transaction, either the buyer or the seller. In the second case, it refers to the amount of money one borrows before interest is charged or accrues.

prorate:
To divide or access anything proportionately. Taxes are often prorated up until the day of closing.

Realtor®:
A broker or salesperson (agent) who is affiliated with the National Association of Realtors. Not all agents are Realtors. The word Realtor (pronounced as two words, Real

TOR) should always be capitalized. It is not free and there is a code of ethics and bylaws that one has to agree to conform to if one is to continue membership.

remainderman:
"The last man standing" in a life estate.

RE/Max agent:
An agent who works for the company known as RE/Max. They differ from most so-called conventional agents in that, in essence, they normally do not split their commissions with the company. They are on what is known as the 100 percent concept (or darned close to it, maybe 95 percent, depending on the state in which they are licensed). They tend to act more like people who are really in business for themselves since they shoulder 100 percent of the risk with respect to advertising and expenses. There are other so-called 100 percent brokers all over North America, but Re/Max is the most popular. They're the ones with the hot air balloon as a logo.

real estate owned (REOs):
Properties that have been taken back by the lender and held in their salvage departments pending future liquidation. Banks are in the lending business. They do not want to own these properties, and many savvy investors can take advantage of this plight by grabbing up these properties for pennies on the dollar.

RESPA statement:
RESPA is another one of those nifty real estate acronyms. It stands for the *Real Estate Settlement and Procedures Act.* The "statement" provides for a precise breakdown of closing costs for both sellers and buyers. RESPA further regulates the specific conduct of mortgage bankers and other lenders as to things they can do or not and how they may advertise. As an

example, lenders cannot pay or receive fees from real estate agents to encourage them to do business with them as opposed to another lender.

restrictive covenant:
A private limitation on the use of real estate that is sometimes included on the recorded deed or subdivision plot. It is binding of all subsequent owners of the property. An example would be where perimeter fences are restricted to no more than six feet in height.

riparian rights:
Not to be confused with water rights, this right extends to an owner of a property bordering a stream or other body of water to continue the use and enjoyment of the waters therein.

settlement:
Also known as the *closing*. It includes all the financial transactions that are required to make the contract final and for title to pass from one owner to the next.

specific performance:
A remedy, under a court order, compelling a defendant to carry out or live up to the terms of an agreement or contract.

statute of frauds:
Legislation requiring that any contract creating or transferring an interest in land or realty be in writing. The intent is to prevent testimony and fraudulent proofs by not allowing oral testimony to alter or vary the terms of the written agreement.

substantive contact:
The first really important dialogue between an agent and a prospective client. At the point of the first substantive

contact, formal disclosure must be made to rid the agent of the problem of undisclosed dual agency.

title:
A document that indicates ownership of property. Titles can be both insurable and marketable. They should be both.

title, chain of:
The succession of all previous title owners all the way back to the first owner.

title, cloud on:
Any outstanding claim or encumbrance which, if determined to be valid, would affect or impair an owner's title. This could take the form of any lien, judgment, or mortgage.

title insurance:
This kind of insurance protects either the lender or the owner or both against any legal defects in the title.

title search:
A detailed examination of the entire document history of a property title to make sure that there are no legal encumbrances.

Torrens system:
A method of title registration in which a clear title is established with a government authority. That authority subsequently issues a certificate to the owner as evidence of their claims.

VA:
The Veterans Administration, a federal government agency that helps veterans in obtaining houses, primarily by guaranteeing loans with super low down payments. These are commonly called VA mortgages.

value:

Any reasonable estimation of worth. In real estate various kinds of value are used, some of which may have nothing to do with another. These kinds of value include:

appraised: The value as determined by a qualified appraiser, typically based on market value using historical data.

assessed: The value for tax purposes established by an assessor based on some sort of formulation of full or partial market value.

market: The kind of valuation that agents and brokers are most concerned with. It is established not by opinion but by what a buyer is willing to pay for a property.

insured: The value that a property can be insured for. Sometimes this value can exceed what is determined to be market or appraised value.

replacement: The actual cost of what it would take to replace (the structure) on a property. Many times this can differ from all other types of valuation.

vendor:

The seller.

water rights:

A right to a stipulated amount of water from a stream, lake, or reservoir.

Appendix 2

Suggested Reading

Carnegie, Dale. *How to Win Friends and Influence People*. New York: Pocket Books, 1994.

Glink, Ilyce R. *100 Questions Every First-Time Home Buyer Should Ask*. New York: Times Books, 2000.

Hopkins, Tom. *How to Master the Art of Selling*. New York: Warner Books, 1982.

Lewis, Byron and R. Frank Pucelick. *Magic of NLP Demystified*. Portland, OR: Metamorphous Press, 1991.

Molloy, William J. *The Complete Home Buyer's Bible*. Hoboken, NJ: John Wiley & Sons, 1996.

Mungo, Ray and Robert H. Yamaguchi. *No Credit Required: How to Buy a House When You Don't Qualify for a Mortgage*. New York: New American Library, 1993.

Murphy, John D. *Secrets of Successful Selling*. New York: Prentice-Hall, 1956.

Ring, Alfred A. and Jerome Dasso. *Real Estate Principles and Practices*. New York: Prentice-Hall, 1977.

Slutsky, Jeff. *How to Get Clients*. New York: Warner Books, 1992.

Trump, Donald with Tony Schwartz. *Trump: The Art of the Deal*. New York: Warner Books, 1989.

Wickman, Floyd and Terri Sjodin. *Mentoring*. New York: McGraw-Hill, 1997.

Index

deposits
earnest money, 12–13, 17,
73–74, 144–145
second, failure to pay, 19,
147–148
depreciation, 44, 57
digital personalities, 96, 98
discrimination, regulations,
36, 58, 161–164
disputes, resolving, 185–192
divorce, as incentive to sell,
37, 67
double dipping, 80
down payments, liquidated
damages and, 12, 17
down payments, little or no
money
about, 76–77, 126–127
assumable mortgages,
128–129
bifurcated financing, 131–133
closing costs, 134, 136
equity sharing, 134
first-time buyer incentives,
38, 76–77
rent to own, 129–130
REO properties, 133–134
seller financing, 130
sweat equity, 130–131
trading assets for, 134–135
VA mortgages, 77, 127–128

E
electro-magnetic field
inspections, 30
equity erosion, 44, 61–62
equity sharing, 134
escrow accounts, 17, 19, 148–150
estate sales, 37, 67
ethics
of principals, 2–6, 11–14,
32, 59–60

of real estate agents, ix–xi,
24–25
exclusive agency
relationships, 63

F
Fair Housing Act, 161–164
fair housing regulations, 36,
161–164
Federal Housing
Administration (FHA), 27,
122, 161–164
fees paid by buyers
appraisals, 18
assumption fees, 129
home inspections, 72–73,
75, 120
junk fees, 177
loan applications, 27
soft costs, 134, 136
fees paid by sellers, 35
For Sale by Owner. *See* FSBO
properties
fiduciaries, defined, 23
financing
bifurcated, 131–133
lending protocols, 141
by owner, 128–129, 130,
131–133, 179
See also down payments;
mortgages
financing problems
brokers' role, 53
delays by lenders, 152
FSBO properties, 51
nonrefundable deposits
and, 73
prequalified loans, 20, 152–153
financing, qualifying for
brokers' role, 51, 83
community buyers
programs, 135

About the Author

Brendan J. Cunningham has been in the real estate business for well over twenty years. In that time as a broker he has personally sold and or brokered more than $1 billion worth of property, which has run the gamut from vacant land to condominiums, from residential to commercial. He received his undergraduate degree in psychology and sociology from S.U.N.Y. at Stonybrook and is currently completing his master's in leadership and organizational change at Daemen College. Prior to immersing himself in real estate, he was a working New York actor. In his spare time, you will see him doing t'ai chi or attempting to play golf as an act of penance somewhere near his home in the tiny hamlet of Griffins Mills, seven miles East of Orchard Park (the home of the Buffalo Bills), where he lives with his wife Kathleen, his daughter Alice, and a rambunctious Sheltie named Mr. Reilly.

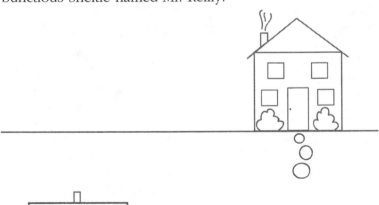